'IN CARRIE'S FOOTPRINTS

THE LONG WALK OF WARREN DORSEY

by Jack McBride White
with Warren Dorsey

ASHLEIGH-REID, PUBLISHERS

In Carrie's Footprints: The Long Walk of Warren Dorsey
Ashleigh-Reid, Publishers
First Edition 2014
Second Update July 2017

Copyright © 2014 by John J. White, Jr.

ISBN: 0963603167

Cover Design: Andrea White
Cover Photo: Carrie Dorsey at top, Warren Dorsey at bottom
(All photos provided by courtesy of the Dorsey family)

www.arpubs.com

DEDICATION
For my mother, Carrie Dorsey
~Warren Dorsey

For Warren and Carolyn Dorsey
~Jack White

CONTENTS

In Carrie's Footprints

The Long Walk of Warren Dorsey

THE MEETING

Let me tell you how I met Warren and came to write this story. I moved to Maryland in 1987, fresh from a year in Japan, where I worked as a civilian on an American airbase, after three years in Germany as a member of the army. A year later, a young woman from Plymouth, Massachusetts, named Andrea Reid moved to Baltimore to live with her sister.

Four years after my arrival, and three years after hers, Andrea and I met in a place called Fells Point in Baltimore. Not many months later, she moved into my small townhouse in Baltimore County and brought along her two cats. Somehow we picked up another cat, a cocker spaniel, a marriage certificate, and a daughter, and things got crowded.

One day I read an article in the *Baltimore City Paper* about a town I'd never heard of and a man I'd never heard of. The town was Sykesville and the man was Jonathan Herman. Herman was mayor of Sykesville and the article, by Bob Allen, described Herman's struggles to revive the old town. I showed Andrea the article, and we drove out for a look.

Sykesville's just over the Patapsco River, heading north as you cross from Howard County over the water and the railroad tracks into Carroll County. The river there seems more like a stream than an actual river. It's shallow and narrow and it takes five seconds to cross the bridge.

And once you're over the water and the tracks, you look up and you're somewhere else, somewhere weird, somewhere like you've never seen before. First off, what's the year? It might be 1870. It might be 1914. But it's definitely the past, and it still looks pretty much exactly how it looked 100 years ago, except the streets are paved now and lined with cars, instead of muddy and lined with horses and carriages. And there are electric lights.

But the train station, the old stone store, the two-block Main Street, the three big buildings on Main Street, the gothic mansion up the hill, the Catholic church on another hill, most everything is almost exactly what you would have seen a century ago.

There might be flat screens in the bar showing baseball and hockey, the train station might be a restaurant, the buildings might have WiFi, but on the outside, you've arrived in a time and a place where you can imagine the local boys heading out to fight the Kaiser's armies in France and all around town nothing but acres and acres of farm and horse country.

When I read the article, Sykesville had recently opened a couple new subdivisions on farmland at the outer reaches of town, and soon enough we bought a nice single family home on four-tenths of an acre.

We thought it would be fun to live in a town with a history and a Main Street and some cool old buildings. Eventually, we started a website called Sykesville Online and I started writing about the town, and one day, thinking I might write a story about it, I visited the town's Historic Sykesville Colored Schoolhouse for an event with three old people I'd never heard of. It was 2011 and we'd been here more than a decade by then.

I knew almost nothing about the schoolhouse. It was one of the things restored when Sykesville revived itself in the late eighties and nineties, but it wasn't something that caught my interest. It was hidden away from the rest of town, a short walk from Main Street, up a steep hill called Oklahoma Avenue, then down a side street off that called Schoolhouse Road, which came to a dead end at a bunch of apartments originally built as public housing in the nineties that now housed Sykesville's hidden, unknown black population.

If you weren't looking for the schoolhouse, you weren't going to find it, and if you didn't stray up there for some reason, and it was hard to stray up there by accident, you would never have known Sykesville had this small black community tucked away up a hill by the river, or that it had been there as long as the town itself.

I walked into the schoolhouse a little late and sat in an old desk that was probably as old as the school itself. A nice woman named Pat Greenwald, who managed the schoolhouse as a sort of museum, rang a big hand bell and gave a brief introduction.

She told us the schoolhouse was built in 1904, around the time Sykesville officially incorporated as a town. She told us it was originally 24 by 16 feet with six windows and two outhouses. She told us there was only the one room, there was no bathroom or electricity or much in the way of light or heat. She told us that only black kids came and how not that long ago it was a crumbling wreck Sykesville's mayors routinely promised to rip down but never quite did.

Up on the slightly raised platform where the teachers used to stand were two women and a man. They were Mae Dorsey Whiten, Warren Dorsey, and Rosie Dorsey Hutchinson, ages 93, 91, and 86. Their mom was the daughter of a slave, and they'd all attended school in this room a very long time ago.

So I listened to the Dorseys. I learned that they'd lived on a small semblance of a farm up the hill near the school. I learned that they tried to live off the land, never had enough money, and used eggs to barter with white merchants in town for things like sugar they couldn't grow or make for themselves. I learned that their mother did wash for white women and their father cooked at the nearby mental hospital.

I learned that early in the twentieth century, there was a black community up there on Oklahoma Hill, living on the edge at the edge of Sykesville, hidden away, and mostly ignored by the white folks.

I learned that Rosie started school a year early, when she was only five, not because she wanted to, but because her older sister Catherine wouldn't go to school without her. I learned that Rosie skipped the second and fourth grades and went off to college alone at 15 and rarely ever came home, because the family couldn't afford the bus fare.

She wasn't old enough to be admitted to college, but as she put it, "The principal and the president of the college got together one day, and I was 15 one minute and then I was 16."

And soon enough she was 19 and a college graduate and teaching elementary school in Frederick, Maryland, to kids barely younger than herself.

And I heard Warren say, "We suffered here. Rosie suffered here. Mae suffered here. I suffered here."

And then he sang for us with the big deep beautiful voice of a five-foot-seven giant.

I wrote my story. The Dorseys liked it. The next time the family came to town, Warren asked me to help write the story of his life, and I agreed. I didn't get started till late August of 2013, and soon enough Warren was 93, and I wanted to make sure if I was going to write his story, he was going to read it. So I wrote fast. I didn't have time to do the great detailed research that historians do. So I didn't. I dug as deep or shallow as need be to make the story good without making it perfect.

I read a lot about American history, about slavery and the Civil War and the civil rights movement and the American South in the first half of the twentieth century. I was shocked by what I learned. And all the while I kept thinking I could research this stuff forever, but I've got to write this book in one year, because as my daughter Anna put it, "You have a deadline. You just don't know when it is."

Warren lives in Frederick, maybe a 40-minute ride from my house, and we met on occasion, but mostly we spoke by computer using Skype. If you don't know what Skype is, just picture him sitting in front of his computer and me sitting in front of mine. Each computer has a camera and a microphone, and we can see and hear each other. I asked questions. He answered them. And I recorded the conversations.

It's easy once you get it set up, but that took us awhile. One day his camera was on the floor and I heard his voice and watched his socks, and sometimes the connection cut in and out, or his image or mine froze on the screen.

But eventually we got good at it, and the 93-year-old black guy with his 91-year-old wife beside him and the 59-year-old white guy sitting at his Mac became friends and worked this thing out together. Screen-to-screen, face-to-face, enjoying each other's company from 20 miles away.

Warren's not a famous person, and his life is not a tragic one filled with dramatic events. Warren didn't change the world. What he did was survive, overcome some very tough odds, and dedicate his life to carrying out his mother's dream that someday her children would lead a better life than hers, that someday they would escape the farm in Sykesville, get educated, and do good things.

And they did. Her name was Carrie, and it's because of her that you're reading this story.

THE FARMER AND THE NIGGER

Let's start in the hayfield. It's 1937, and there's a boy and a man, and they're out in the field at the end of a late summer day. The boy's 16. He's tired and dusty and dirty from working all day with a pitchfork. The farmer's a tall, white, weather-beaten old guy in his sixties or seventies, wearing overalls and a straw hat.

He was probably born in Maryland, probably not long after the Civil War, most likely in the 1870s, when blacks were freshly freed, the South was smoldering, and the country was putting itself together again after the greatest tragedy in its history.

The boy weighs 140 pounds. He's not tall and not wearing a hat or proper underwear. He's worn patched-together hand-me-downs all his life. The family has a small farm and some chickens. His mom makes the underwear from the sacks the chicken feed comes in.

The boy's just out of high school and tired from working in the sun harvesting hay, but he has a plan and needs every cent he can get. Now he's ready to move the plan from one stage to the next.

He tells the farmer, "Looks like I'll be quitting."

The farmer's surprised. The boy's a hard worker. He's cheap labor. He's lean and strong and tireless. He's serious and no trouble at all.

The farmer asks, "Why you want to do that?"

"Going to college."

"College? What for?"

"I don't know. Thought maybe I'd like to teach."

The farmer bends down a bit. The brim of his straw hat shades his face. He squints straight into the boy's eyes then dispenses some advice.

"Boy, you know a nigger ain't got sense enough to teach."

Sykesville's a town of some 4000 people today, out in the country, northwest of Baltimore, not far from the city, just 20 miles away for a crow or a pigeon. By car on a Sunday afternoon, you can get to Baltimore's Inner Harbor in half an hour or go the other way and make it to Washington, D.C., in probably an hour, depending on traffic and road conditions and your driving skills.

The boy in the hayfield was born in Sykesville in 1920 in the family house on the family farm up Oklahoma Hill. He was born on November 17 in a place with no electricity, no running water, and no heat other than what came off the stove in the kitchen where they burned wood they cut on their land.

The boy's mom had been young and beautiful once. Her name was Carrie. She was 34, and this was her ninth child in 16 years.

Carrie's mother's name was Catherine, but everyone called her Aunt Kitty, and it was Aunt Kitty who delivered the baby. Aunt Kitty delivered all Carrie's babies up to that point, but this was the first in the farmhouse and first that didn't look like he would make it.

Aunt Kitty looked like a white woman, but she wasn't exactly. She'd grown up a slave in a compound not far from Sykesville. She was very good at delivering babies, but this baby was small and hardly breathing and most likely not going to survive his first night. Since there weren't any doctors available for these poor black women, the women were on their own. So they took turns watching the baby and praying.

The baby survived the first night. And then another. They gave him constant attention, but they never gave him a name. So probably, they didn't expect him to make it.

Then Professor Lee showed up. Professor Lee was a teacher, or a prophet, or a mythical creature all rolled into one, to everyone who knew him. But nobody really knew him. Nobody knew his true name or where he came from. He was just a black man called Professor Lee.

He arrived unexpectedly that day. He'd known Carrie since she was little. He'd known her husband, Ed Dorsey, too. They'd both grown up in a rundown settlement of shacks and outhouses and small farms on some scrubby land in a place near Cooksville about five miles south of

Sykesville, where once in 1863, Confederate cavalry under General J.E.B. Stuart won a brief skirmish with some Maryland militia.

Professor Lee was their first teacher, their only teacher really, in the academic sense, and he'd come to visit just by chance, and there was the baby, and Professor Lee asked if he could name him.

There'd recently been an election, and Professor Lee named the baby after the new president, Warren Gamaliel Harding. Through his life, most people would call him Tom, but his real name, conferred by the visiting Professor Lee, became Warren Gamaliel Dorsey.

Not long after naming Warren, Professor Lee said goodbye and left the Dorsey farm. They never saw him again.

THE EDUCATION

The Dorseys lived on their farm up near the schoolhouse, Ed, Carrie, and 12 children, but never all at once. The big kids would grow up and move away, and new ones would come along to replace them.

In the early days, before the school opened in 1904, if you were black and a kid, you didn't go to school. You learned what you could from your parents, and they hadn't been to school, either, so you didn't learn much. There were hundreds of one-room schools for white kids scattered about rural Maryland, and even the white kids seldom got beyond the seven grades of elementary.

Ed learned some math and a bit of reading from Professor Lee and learned everything else on his own. Carrie couldn't read or write well, and her children were probably destined for the same fate. But three fathers from Oklahoma Hill journeyed to the county seat in Westminster, 18 miles away, and asked the Carroll County Board of Education to build them a school.

The timing was good. Maryland had recently mandated that every school district provide a free education to every child. In 1896, in the case of *Plessy v. Ferguson*, the United States Supreme Court ruled that as long as facilities for the races were equal, they could be separate.

They never defined equal, but Carroll County defined it as what they eventually built on that hill after the Board of Education surprised those three fathers and agreed with their request.

Warren says, "The Supreme Court established this principle of separate but equal, but they didn't determine who can decide what's equal. The county, operating under the law as they interpreted it, noted that the school was separate, and they determined it was equal. They said, 'You got a school; the white kids got a school. You got books, although they were used books; they got books.' They determined that was equal."

In her good and handy book, *Sykesville Past and Present: A Walking Tour*, Linda Greenberg writes that they built the school from wood for just more than $530 on an acre of land they bought from Asa Hepner, a man most distinguished by a gigantic moustache, whose photo adorns the schoolhouse today. The land wasn't much good to him, sloping straight down toward the river and the railroad tracks, and most likely he was happy to get rid of it.

Hepner was Sykesville's second mayor and long-time postmaster. He owned what he referred to as a "Music Emporium" on Main Street, where, according to one of his ads in the *Sykesville Herald*, you could get a good "second-hand square piano for $20," a "fine second-hand organ for $18," and listen to the latest records for your Victrola before you bought them.

Besides musical instruments, Hepner owned houses, including just about everything up Oklahoma Hill. Warren calls him the original slumlord, because he rented out his shacks but did nothing to maintain them.

It's a mystery how Sykesville, in the middle of all that farmland owned by white people, ended up with a black neighborhood tucked away behind its Main Street, but most likely it had to do with farming and slavery.

Virginia was the first American colony to import slaves and build its economy on their labor, but Maryland wasn't far behind. Slaves started arriving in Maryland in 1642, and by 1664, marriage between the white and black races was illegal, slaves were ruled slaves for life, and the children of slaves were also slaves for life. As Maryland evolved into a tobacco colony based on plantations and the free labor of unfree Africans, slavery became common and vital.

By the mid-eighteenth century, there were nearly 150,000 people in Maryland; approximately 40 percent were African slaves, and by 1753, according to Maryland law, you couldn't set free one of your slaves even if you wanted to. The freeing of slaves, referred to as "manumission," remained illegal till 1796.

By the Civil War, a lot of whites had freed their slaves, and after the war, they had no choice. Since there were once plenty of slaves around Sykesville, there were now a lot of freed slaves looking for work and a place to live.

Most wandered off toward Baltimore, but a few remained behind and did day labor cheap on the area's many farms, and 50 to 60 years after the slaves gained their freedom, some of their descendants began moving up into Hepner's homes. As blacks moved in and whites moved out, a small poor black community developed and eventually built their school.

The county provided no transportation, but the kids came from miles around, however they could get there. The Dorseys were lucky. They stepped out the door and arrived at school a couple minutes later.

Warren started in 1926 and remembers it like yesterday. Planks on the floor. Rough walls without any paint. Books with pages torn out by white kids who owned them first. Old desks with initials carved in by white kids who owned them first. A bunch of kids ages six to 12 crammed into a room with one underpaid teacher who rode the train in from Baltimore each day. A dipper they passed around with water from the nearby Dorsey family stream. Heat from a coal stove that sometimes coated the windows with soot and could never quite get the room warm enough on cold windy days.

They wore their coats in class and breathed in the coal dust that coated the glass and the floors and their hands.

Warren says, "It was a minimal effort to provide educational opportunities for African-American children. It was only done to shut up these couple rabble-rousers in the community. If it had been their intention to educate us, they would have given us decent books. They didn't. They would have supplied decent furniture. They didn't. They gave us cast-offs, hand-me-downs. But to us, who had nothing, it was the first glimmer of hope for a better tomorrow."

The teacher's name was Gertrude Johnson. She was nice and popular with the kids and parents but not really a trained teacher and most likely unqualified for the job. She got up early every day, got in the colored car, and rode the rails in from Baltimore. By the time she walked up the long steep hill to the school, she was often late and always tired. And for the most part, she didn't teach all that much.

She alternated teaching first, third, fifth, and seventh grades one day, and second, fourth, and sixth the next. On their off-days, the kids taught each other. Warren barely learned a thing.

But in the middle of his year in fifth grade, the county decided to consolidate schools. Warren and Mae got transferred to a school in Johnsville, four miles north of Sykesville, where another of those small, intriguing black communities had popped up in the farmland.

Now instead of stepping out the door and arriving at school a few minutes later, they had to travel miles, and of course, once again, the county didn't provide transportation.

"So often, we ended up walking," he says. "And it would take us an hour, an hour and a half, along a public highway to get to school, exposing us to all manner of weather and the constant threat of motorized traffic."

It was another all-black school with no running water and a potbelly stove for heat, but this one had twice the rooms and twice the teachers. In other words, two of each.

Warren says, "One teacher had first, second, and third grades, the second had fourth, fifth, sixth, and seventh. That was Miss Bell, and we thought she was an ogre. She was probably in her forties, but we thought she was ancient, and she was a domineering character in the classroom.

"But she taught me to read. Because when I went there I had very poor reading skills, and after being with her that year and a half I did pretty well. I didn't really like the lady. But in retrospect, she was a lifesaver. Whatever she said, you did it, or she used her yardstick to get her message across.

"And she had a passion for educating those kids and making sure we were citizens of this country, that regardless of how we were treated, we were citizens here."

She wanted the kids to learn, and if they didn't want to learn she was going to make them learn. Warren gets it now. Her heart was good. She wouldn't accept failure. But back then, he dreaded her.

He says, "Miss Bell used to have a spelling bee every Friday, and everybody was lined up, and you had your spelling list for the week. And you go through the line, and if you missed the word, you got whacked. But that didn't eliminate you.

"She put you at the end of the line to come through a second time. Well I was then, and still am, a notorious bad speller, and if I missed a word I got whacked. Yes indeed, sometimes on a Friday I might get whacked more than once. And it didn't feel good."

Warren hated Fridays, but ancient old Miss Bell taught Warren something he'd managed to miss in five years in Sykesville's Colored Schoolhouse.

"In retrospect, the best thing that ever happened to me was Miss Bell, because I learned to read, and you'll be amazed what an effect that had. We had no books at home, but with the books available mostly at school, I could learn about other places, other cultures, other kids. There was a world beyond the little place where I lived, and this was a tremendous revelation."

Carroll County opened its first high school in Westminster in 1899. It was whites only and not many went. If you were black, you got to Baltimore, or you were done. But in 1928, the county slapped together some WWI army barracks in Westminster and created a school for black students. They called it Robert Moton High School.

In those days, there were seven grades of elementary and four of high school, but in Warren's world, elementary was the end, if you made it. He heard of Robert Moton, but there was no way to get there.

In fact, hardly anyone could get there. Kids were scattered all over the place. So the principal decided to buy a bus to round up students. Except he didn't have any money. But somehow the county's black community pulled enough together for a down payment.

The bus was run-down and freezing in winter. The seats lined up along the walls instead of one behind the other. They found a teacher to drive it. He lived in

Cooksville, and every day he drove from Cooksville through towns named Mount Airy and Taylorsville and Eldersburg and eventually to Westminster, picking up small groups of poor country blacks along the way. He drove for free.

James Norris and Harry Rheubottom, from the Sykesville area, decided to give high school a try. They would walk a few miles to Eldersburg, catch the bus, and ride out to Robert Moton. Warren and Mae wanted to join them, but there was one problem.

Warren says, "Since the county didn't supply the bus, didn't supply a driver, didn't supply any maintenance or any money for gas, each kid was assessed 50 cents a week. My mother didn't have the dollar. Then toward the end of September, my sister Thelma, who lived in Baltimore, decided she could come up with a dollar a week.

"And around the first of October, Mae and I joined forces with James and Harry to become the first foursome from the Sykesville Colored Schoolhouse to attend high school in Carroll County.

"The man who owned the school bus franchise for white kids, and brought them to the school in Sykesville, lived in the New Windsor area. And if we happened to be on the road when he came past, he'd pick us up in his empty bus and haul us out to Eldersburg without charging anything, so occasionally we got a ride that way.

"And we got rides every now and then otherwise, mostly from whites. They saw these kids walking along the road and would pick us up. One other guy, an African American who drove a farm delivery truck for the Maryland Milling and Supply Company, a guy named Hagen Bond, he often picked us up. I think if he had any customers out that way, he made sure he was traveling about the same time as us."

So sometimes they got rides. Sometimes they walked more than three miles on a dangerous road in all kinds of weather. They walked north on Route 32, which was narrower than it is today, and even today there are no sidewalks, and it's dangerous enough that crashes are common and occasionally people die or get flown off in helicopters. Most of the cars that drove by ignored the four black kids lugging their schoolbags out to Eldersburg, but if a school bus went by, the white kids would shout things of an unkind nature out the windows.

There were other problems. Some of them funny. For instance, their father made Mae wear a pair of black bloomers to school in winter. They were meant for sports, not for wearing around. Mae much preferred arriving at school in cold legs to these ugly black bloomers.

So each day, shortly after leaving home, she slipped her bloomers over her shoes and hung them in a tree. After school, just short of home, she took the bloomers off the tree and put them back on. Ed never suspected, her three male companions never said a word, and eventually all four made it through high school.

With a little math, which is something he's quite good at, Warren calculates that walking three years out to Johnsville to finish up grammar school, and a few more to Eldersburg to catch the bus to Robert Moton, attending school 180 days a year, Warren and Mae probably walked about 10,000 miles apiece and barely missed a day.

It was 1933 when Warren started high school. He still lived with pigs and chickens, the family cow, and Frank, whom he loved very much and was a horse. He still slept on a bed stuffed with straw and wore underpants with the name of a feed manufacturer on them.

For breakfast he ate corn cakes, what he calls a sort of flapjack made out of corn meal and covered with syrup. For lunch he ate slices of bread stuck together with more syrup, and thanks to Miss Bell, his mother's encouragement, a serious determination, and two excellent teachers at Robert Moton, Warren not only ate a lot of syrup, he also learned to read. He got good at it.

And four years later, something surprising happened. You can read about it online today in the June 18, 1937, edition of the *Carroll County Times*, under this heading, "Robert Moton School Holds Commencement Exercises."

"...Mrs. Paul M. Wimert, President of the American Legion Auxiliary, made the presentation of the Auxiliary medal to Warren Gamaliel Dorsey as the outstanding student of the senior class."

Warren finished on top. He was valedictorian. And Maryland was giving out scholarships to a state college of your choice to the top student in each high school in the state. Of course, for Warren that meant a black state college of his choice. Warren got one of those scholarships and something nearly impossible occurred to him: "Maybe I can go to college."

Except the scholarship was just $50, less than half what he needed, and that's how Warren ended up on the hayfield that day with the pitchfork and the farmer. He stood right at the edge of a miracle. All he needed was a bit of money, good health, and for the world to not fall apart.

But it was 1937, and both his health and the world were about to fall apart.

Above: Emerson, Mae, Warren and doll in front of the schoolhouse in 1927. Mae says, "That doll was everything."

Left: Rosie and Catherine posing in their neckties.

Above: Mae, Rosie, Catherine, and Thelma in Sam and Thelma's first car, circa 1939.

Left: Warren in his Sunday best in 1927, the day of the wooden cake.

FREEDOM

The town of Sykesville is named after James Sykes, an Englishman brought by his parents to Baltimore at a very young age. He fought against England in the Battle of Baltimore in September 1814, probably heard, or even saw, the bombs bursting in air that Francis Scott Key wrote about, and sometime in the 1820s, he arrived in the area that later became Sykesville. He bought a rundown gristmill and converted it into the Howard Cotton Factory just as the Baltimore & Ohio Railroad ran a line through the area.

It was a great location. On the river, the railroad coming through, perfectly set between the textile markets in the North and cotton fields in the South, where blacks worked 14-hour days in the blistering sun with the whip at their backs. He imported skilled workers from England and made them houses beside the mill and the river.

He built a giant hotel with 47 rooms that filled, each summer, with tourists from Baltimore who came to escape the heat, stink, and disease of the filthy city. He ran his factory, bought land and a few slaves, prospered even, but then came financial troubles in the 1850s, and eventually he sold his hotel to a man named Grimes.

Before the Civil War, the area around Sykesville was known as the Freedom District and still is today. The town itself was very small and sparsely populated, but large farms owned by a few wealthy landowners dominated the area surrounding it.

And despite its name, if you were black, valued your freedom, and lived in Carroll County, Freedom was the last place you wanted to be, and freedom was something you were most unlikely to possess.

According to the 1840 census, there were 1122 slaves in Carroll County and 445 lived in the Freedom District. In the Freedom District, there were 1723 people, and 26 percent were slaves, one slave for every three white people.

Freedom was fifth in population, first in black population, and first in slavery.

A man named George Patterson owned more slaves than anyone. Patterson is kind of a tragic figure, if not necessarily a likable one. He married late, and his only son died just short of Christmas in 1849. The son's name was George Patterson, Jr. He was only five, and it's not likely his father, who was 53, ever recovered from the loss.

Patterson was a hard man, a successful dairy farmer, and almost certainly a Confederate sympathizer, who ran a huge plantation known as Springfield and refused to free his many slaves until forced to.

He's also a footnote in the much larger tale of his famous sister Betsy Patterson, who married Napoleon Bonaparte's younger brother Jerome against her father's wishes in 1803.

Betsy and George were two of William Patterson's 12 children. William Patterson, who was one of the wealthiest men in post-Revolution America, made a great deal of money supplying George Washington's army. He built Springfield as a summer escape from Baltimore. George inherited it from his father, turned it into a lush and profitable plantation, and ran it for decades.

When George died, he left the land to his daughter, Florence. When Florence died at 31 while giving birth to a baby who also died, Patterson's widow, Prudence, and her son-in-law inherited the estate, but grief-stricken and uninterested in maintaining operations, they sold it to a man named Frank Brown in 1880.

Frank Brown was Prudence Patterson's nephew. His father, Stephen Brown, was Prudence's brother. Frank Brown would one day become the only person from Carroll County ever elected governor of Maryland.

His term as governor from 1892 to 1896 was mostly uneventful. Like the Pattersons, Brown owned thousands of acres and grew up surrounded by farmland and slaves, but when his wife died, he also lost interest in land and farming and Sykesville and left it all behind for Baltimore.

He sold the thousand acres he bought from the Pattersons to the state of Maryland for $50,000, and on that land, Maryland built the Springfield Mental Hospital for the

Insane. And it's this hospital that would eventually draw the Dorseys to Sykesville.

Emancipation

Just a couple miles southeast of Sykesville, there's an even smaller place called Marriottsville, and in Marriottsville in the years before the Civil War, there was a small compound they called "Little Africa," run by a man named Isaac Anderson. Anderson was a slave dealer, and one of his slaves was a girl born in 1847, who looked very much like a little white girl.

Between the sixteenth and nineteenth centuries, 12 million Africans crossed the Atlantic in reeking slave ships, mostly crammed below deck, and often chained to one another. They called the trip "the Middle Passage."

The passage took months, and 10 to 20 percent of the human cargo died of murder, starvation, sickness, and suicide during the crossing. Some 10 million made it, another two million didn't.

The United States banned the importation of slaves in 1808. After that, slaves were homegrown, and the domestic trade boomed along with worldwide demand for cotton from the American South. In the first half of the nineteenth century, Maryland, Virginia, and the Carolinas shipped hundreds of thousands of slaves further south.

Isaac Anderson bought slaves on the docks at Annapolis, or elsewhere, then moved them up to the compound in Marriottsville. It's possible he supplied area farmers such as George Patterson and the others who worked the land around Sykesville, but most of his slaves were destined southward, where demand was steady and slaves were expensive.

Isaac was the last of the Andersons, and the little girl was Warren's grandmother, Catherine, who they would later call Aunt Kitty. Anderson sold three of her siblings, but he never sold her.

And although Kitty looked like a white girl, her mother, Harriet Fletcher, was a brown-skinned woman who shared her bed with a black man named Bob Tyler, who probably would have married her if Anderson let him.

Harriet was Isaac Anderson's slave. So was Tyler. So was Kitty.

Warren says, "Bob Tyler was his man in charge. He kept the slaves in line when Isaac wasn't around and operated the blacksmith shop. Isaac liked to pretend to be absent to see whether Bob had the slaves under control, and if he caught them doing what they shouldn't, he whipped them. One night he'd been gone a long time, and the slaves pulled together what they could and Anderson caught them having a sort of party.

"Bob had worked hard all day and was sleeping. So the slaves weren't behaving like Isaac required, and he told Bob, 'I'll deal with you in the morning.' The next morning, Bob was in his blacksmith shop, and Isaac appeared with a whip. Bob picked up his blacksmithing hammer and said, 'The day you lay that whip on me is the day you die.'

"Anderson told him, 'You're going south on the next shipment.' But he never got rid of him because he needed him."

By 1860, one in seven Americans was a slave. Most lived in reeking disease-ridden shacks with dirt floors, where often they suffered from dysentery, tuberculosis, malaria, pneumonia, typhus, and cholera. They worked 14 or 15 hours a day. They were frequently whipped. If they fell under the heat and strain of picking cotton all day, they were whipped back into action or whipped until senseless or even dead.

Pregnant women worked the fields till it became impossible. The average weight of a slave baby was five and a half pounds. Half died. Those who didn't, became slaves at birth. By seven or eight, when they hit the cotton fields, they likely had worms, rotten teeth, and not very long to live.

The various colonies and then states had their own slave codes. You could place a slave as a bet, use a slave for collateral on a loan, offer a slave as a gift, pass slaves down from generation to generation, split slave families up in your will.

South Carolina's slave code as published in 1740 declared that murdering your own slave would be punishable by a fine of 700 pounds, killing a slave in a fit of passion or while correcting the slave would cost you 350 pounds, and castrating, scalding, burning, cutting out the tongue, putting out the eye, or removing a slave's limb or other body part would cost you 100 pounds.

It was forbidden by law to inflict any cruel punishment on a slave "other than whipping or beating with a horse-whip, cow-skin, switch or small stick, or by putting irons on, or confining or imprisoning such slave." And because, "the having of slaves taught to write, or suffering them to be employed in writing, may be attended with great inconveniences, teaching slaves to write would be punishable by a 100-pound fine for every offense." Castrating a slave, cutting out his tongue, or teaching him to read were all punished equally under the law.

Many states modeled their codes after those of Virginia. The Virginia codes declared that slaves "shall be held to be real estate." And that if you killed a slave while dispensing discipline for poor behavior, "the master shall be free of all punishment...as if such accident never happened."

While Kitty was still a teenager, Anderson made a deal with a black man named John T. Dorsey. Born in 1837, John Dorsey was a free man, 10 years older than Kitty, and Anderson agreed that in exchange for a certain amount of work over time, Dorsey could eventually purchase Kitty's freedom and marry her.

When Abraham Lincoln issued his proclamation freeing the slaves in 1863, it did not free Kitty. It freed only those slaves in states in active rebellion against the United States. It did not free the slaves in Maryland, Missouri, Delaware, and Kentucky, slave states that hadn't betrayed the Union.

In 1864, when Maryland amended its constitution and freed its slaves, Kitty walked off Isaac Anderson's compound, young, smart, and free, probably assuming she would never again see the man who'd owned her through her entire life.

But one day many years later, sometime during the First World War when Kitty was near 70, she did see him again. Anderson had never married. He'd held Kitty 17 years a slave, sold away her family, took advantage of her mother, and as he lay dying, very old, and probably alone, 50 years after their parting, he called for the slave girl he hadn't seen since the days of Abraham Lincoln and Robert E. Lee.

"He was on his deathbed," Warren says. "And she came and stayed with him until he died. And I'm sure she knew very well that this was her father, and he knew very well that this was his daughter."

Bush Park

Around the time Kitty went free, some former slave owners in the part of Howard County known as Cooksville set aside some land where their freed slaves could set up homes. Warren calls the small plot "bush land," and on this bit of land they named Bush Park, or Bushy Park, a small black community scraped out a living.

It wasn't good land or a very good living. The men who once owned the slaves kept the good land for themselves and set up their former slaves as a labor pool they could tap for low wages and nothing in the way of benefits or promise or rights or respect. Just a bit of work and a bit of money on an as-needed basis.

The deal between Isaac Anderson and John Dorsey could not have been binding now that the slaves were free people, but however she might have felt about it, and despite the fact that Dorsey hadn't yet worked enough hours to complete the purchase, Catherine married John in 1866. They settled in Bush Park, built a four-room house, and raised 12 kids.

In the 1870s, farmers raised crops and took them to open-air markets in Baltimore, and John worked for these farmers as a teamster. He drove his team of horses to Baltimore on Fridays, sold the crops on Saturdays, and came home on Sundays.

He never earned more than 12 dollars a month, but he found other ways to make do. He had a patch of land. He raised wheat that eventually became a barrel of whole-wheat flour. He raised corn for corn meal. He raised pigs, butchered them, and cured them with salt. He caught and salted enough fish to fill a barrel. He raised vegetables. They ate what they needed and canned the rest. They put away their meat and fish and vegetables for the winter.

They were a very good team. John was a provider. Kitty was good in other ways. She became a key figure in the Bush Park community.

When people had babies, when they were sick or dying, there were no doctors, there was no health care, there was no medicine, there was nowhere to turn outside Bush

Park, and so they turned to Aunt Kitty, and she became what Warren calls, "the medicine woman."

He says, "She knew plant, herbal, and root remedies. She learned to tend the sick and comfort a family mourning the loss of a loved one. And she learned to deliver babies. She learned all that as a slave and brought it with her when she was freed."

Whenever anyone got sick in Bush Park, they called her. Whenever anyone died in Bush Park, they called her. In her later years, Kitty served as a midwife to white women and stayed with them during the weeks after their babies were born.

At one point, she made good use of her relationship with these white women to develop her own smallpox treatment.

"During a smallpox epidemic she got called by a lot of white women after the children were vaccinated. They would develop a scab, and when the scab came off, Aunt Kitty would collect the scabs. What she did to her own children and others in the community, is she would poke the arm with a needle and put the scab over it, and bind it, and that was the way she vaccinated children."

The people of Bush Park couldn't read or write and had very little chance of learning. They had no marketable skills, almost no employment opportunities, and few real prospects of any sort, except working on farms for men who used to own them or their parents. They were poor and illiterate, and as Warren puts it, "totally dependent upon their intuitive instincts, and the erratic benevolence of their former slave owners."

Then came Professor Lee. He had no family there. He didn't seem to own anything. He didn't seem to want anything. He just wandered into the community and stayed, an educated black man with no known past, walking out of slavery's shadow into this small camp of former slaves and their children.

He taught the kids to read and write. He taught them music. He said there was life beyond Bush Park. He said education was the way out. They didn't have to be poor forever. They were free now and should grab the opportunity and make the most of it.

Warren says, "As a child, I learned about Jesus in Sunday school. And all I've ever learned about unadulterated love for the needy is embodied in my image of Jesus. He came into the lives of the forgotten masses and brought hope and understanding. He brought salvation. He inspired everyone to be like him. He created a world where there would be an endless procession of Jesuses replicating his deeds.

"Was Professor Lee the black Jesus? He came out of nowhere. He disappeared after I was born. He was never heard of since. Was he Jesus reincarnated? Could there be walking all over, many reincarnations of Jesus, based on our image of Jesus the man?"

To Bush Park, Professor Lee was a savior of sorts, and the salvation he promised could only be acquired through education. It was a lesson that would take root in the mind of a poor black girl with light skin and a pretty face. She was Kitty's ninth daughter, and she would become a disciple of Professor Lee and, like him, one of Warren's many Jesus figures, ingraining in her children the notion that hard work and education would set them free.

Her name was Carrie Dorsey, and she too would become a medicine woman of sorts, only not in Bush Park, but years later in another poor isolated black community.

"On Oklahoma Hill, everybody called her 'Miss Carrie,'" Warren says. "If there was sickness, something that seemed a little challenging, or the birth of a baby, who did they call? 'Go get Miss Carrie.' And my mother would go.

"I don't know if she had any great skills that made her a factor, but the people were happy with her. I remember distinctly when one of the Rheubottom boys died, the first person the mother called on was Miss Carrie. Off my mother goes."

Carrie learned caring, compassion, and competence from her mother. She learned the value of education from Professor Lee. She inherited her father's gift for organizing, planning, and providing.

And somewhere back in Bush Park, she met a boy named Ed Dorsey.

And No One Takes Ed

Ed was born in 1884. His family lived mostly around Bush Park, but travelled too, from farm to farm, living in the small shacks farmers provided their workers. Unlike Carrie's family, they never owned a home.

Ed's maternal grandfather was a free man named Madd Savoy, who appeared to be white, but was classified as a mulatto and worked on a farm in Montgomery County, Maryland. The farm owner's granddaughter Mary spent her summers there, and sometime in the first half of the 1800s, Madd Savoy and this young white girl ran off and got married.

When Mary discovered that Madd Savoy had African ancestors, it didn't change anything. They had several children, including one named Georgianna, who like Aunt Kitty, looked just as white as any other white girl and could have passed herself off as one. But she didn't. Instead, she married a black man named Andrew Dorsey, who brought her north from Montgomery County to the area around Bush Park.

Andrew worked where he could find it, mostly day work on farms. Andrew and Georgianna had seven children. Five survived into adulthood. There was Emma, followed by Rose, Ed, Ben, and Hattie. Emma and Rose married in their teens and moved away.

Andrew came and went. No one knew where he went or when he'd come back. He would stay with the family awhile and then disappear again, and at 37, while Andrew was off somewhere, Georgianna passed away.

There were three young kids. Emma took Hattie to her home in Fairmont Heights near Washington, D.C. Rose took Ben to her place near Sykesville. No one took Ed.

It was 1898. Ed was 14. He didn't go hunting for his father. Instead, he hopped freight trains and traveled the rails. He worked farms or wherever else he could find a day's work – Frederick, Maryland; Northern Virginia; somewhere up in Pennsylvania – and eventually, he made his way to southwest Baltimore.

By 1900, Baltimore had half a million people and more than 70,000 were black. There were relatives there, and friends from Bush Park, but not much in the way of opportunities. His mom was dead. His dad was missing. He had no family, no money, and no skills. He never found a home or any sort of permanent residence. He slept where he could, maybe a pool hall or a floor in the house of a friend.

A barber named Jim Prettyman from Bush Park taught him to cut hair. He fixed shoes. He hustled pool. He read whatever he could get his hands on and soon became a very good reader. He slept wherever he could find a place. He lived five years that way, before finally coming home to Bush Park. He was 18, maybe 19, and all those years away, he had never forgotten a very pretty girl he grew up with.

The Road to Sykesville

Ed and Carrie got married sometime around 1903. Carrie was 16. And then the roaming began again. Only soon enough, there was a baby named Clifton roaming with them. They moved from place to place, wherever Ed could find a day's work. Eventually they settled on a dairy farm in Virginia.

Ed worked the farm. Carrie stayed home with the baby. They lived in a house raised on stilts. And one day in the middle of the afternoon while Ed was off in the fields, Carrie heard a noise, like someone rattling the door. But there was no one there. Then it happened again and again.

Finally Ed stayed home to investigate and he heard it too. He looked around. Looked under the house up on its stilts. Nothing.

Maybe they were scared. Maybe they thought it was an omen. Maybe it was destiny calling. They didn't stick around to find out. They rented a wagon and some horses and were off again, back to Maryland. They stopped outside Washington in a place called Muirkirk, Maryland. Ed worked farms again, and Everett was born in 1907.

There were four now. They kept moving, slowly working their way back to Bush Park and eventually settling with Ed's sister Rose and her husband, Gus Rheubottom, not all that far from Bush Park, but closer to Sykesville.

They lived there awhile and then moved again. This time they settled in the town of Sykesville in a house behind the big Main Street store of Marion and Margaret Harris. It wasn't much of a house, more or less a glorified four-room shack, but rent was free as long as Carrie did the wash for the owner's family.

They stayed there awhile and finally in 1915, the Dorseys moved up to a house on Oklahoma Hill and began settling in with Sykesville's black community.

Warren says, "All the houses on Oklahoma Hill were inhabited by white people once. There was a transition going on when my parents moved up. There were only two white families still there, and we bought the one house and Jim Norris bought the other. And Thelma, Romulus, Vernon, Chester, and I think Mae, were all born there."

Ed's oldest sister, Emma (*left*), with Hattie, the sister she raised.

Ed Dorsey at 18 or 19 years of age, around the time he came back for Carrie.

Carrie Dorsey at 16, the year she married Ed.

THE DORSEY MACHINE

In 1868, the Patapsco River flooded, tore down every brick of the hotel built by James Sykes, and took away most of the rest of the town with it. Between the flood of 1868 and 1915, when the Dorseys moved up to Oklahoma Hill, Sykesville rebuilt itself on the other side of the river and became pretty much the town it is today.

After the flood, as the town re-established on the Carroll side of the river, a guy named John Harvey Fowble built things. In 1878, he built the row of stores called the McDonald block on Main Street. In 1884, E. Francis Baldwin built a train station to accommodate passenger trains. And somewhere around the same time, Frank Brown built a winding collection of summer cottages for visitors from Baltimore.

Main Street Sykesville is only two blocks long. Fowble built most of it. He attached an attractive bank building to the end of the McDonald block. He built the present Sykesville Town House, where the town's mayor and town government do their business. And on the second block, referred to as Arcade Place back then, he built the Arcade Building, another bank building, and the Wade H. D. Warfield store, the three old, attractive, and solid buildings that make you think maybe this town used to be someplace. Or at least intended to give it a try.

When the Dorseys moved up the hill, most of the structure of modern Sykesville already existed, and mostly Fowble built it. But Fowble was just an architect and builder. The mastermind behind it all, the visionary businessman who set out to build a great American town and get rich doing it, was Wade Hampton Devries Warfield.

Warfield was born October 7, 1864, and grew up in a mansion just outside Sykesville, where his father ran a large dairy farm. In 1889, at 25, Warfield opened a supply business downtown. He created the Sykesville Lumber, Coal and Grain Company, which later became the Maryland Milling and Supply Company.

In 1901, he started the Sykesville Bank. In 1907, he created the Sykesville Realty and Investment Company. He lured three journalists from Baltimore and started the *Sykesville Herald*. Sykesville incorporated as a town in 1904, and by 1909, while still short of 40, Warfield succeeded Asa Hepner and became the town's third mayor.

He was easily the most powerful businessman in the area, a mayor, and then a state senator, and always a farmer, running at one point what the *Herald* described as "four extensive farms nearby, always in a high state of cultivation."

And then everything went bad. In 1920, a massive fire that lit up the sky for miles destroyed his flourmill at the bottom of Oklahoma Hill, leaving it, as the *Herald* wrote, nothing but "charred timber and ashes." In 1923, Sykesville's second great flood washed away his lumberyard. And then in 1927, two years before the Great Depression, he managed somehow to lose everything he owned.

No one knows exactly what went wrong, but he ended up broke and living in a small home that stands today at 7318 Springfield Avenue in Sykesville, where on June 17, 1935, at the age of 70, Wade Warfield collapsed on his porch and died about a month later.

The *Herald* wrote, "there is not an industrial enterprise in town, and scarcely a home or a family that has not been touched by the kindly, generous spirit of this man, in some intimate way."

But actually there was, and the head of that family was a man named Ed Dorsey.

Ed Buys the Farm

Around 1910, while living with his sister, Rose, Ed finally landed his first actual job, the kind where you show up each day and collect a check every week or two. It was at Springfield Hospital for the Insane just outside Sykesville on the land the Pattersons sold to Frank Brown and Brown sold to the state.

Springfield started accepting patients in 1896, and the population expanded quickly into the thousands. It was white-only and would stay that way till the 1960s, but the kitchens were integrated many years before, and that's where Ed got his job.

He started as a helper, but soon was a cook, and then head of the kitchen. He stayed there more than 10 years and mostly hated it. It seems he wanted respect. Eventually he gave up on that and just wanted out. And he came up with a plan. He would do things the old way, like John Dorsey in Bush Park. Buy a farm, get self-sufficient, and the hell with white people.

A white man named A.C. Brown worked at Springfield as a carpenter, and that's probably where they met. Brown wanted to start a business in town. He had a farm to sell, seven cleared acres, some intervening property, and another 35 acres about half cleared. Ed could have it, the house, the land, the buildings, the animals, for $3200.

It was a lot for a 36-year-old cook with eight kids, but Ed knew how to manage his money. He had $1000. All he needed was another $2200. But despite the cash, despite the collateral the house and land and buildings represented, despite that he'd held a steady job at a reliable place the past 10 years, in 1920 no one in Sykesville, including Wade Warfield, would lend $2200 to a black man.

But Ed got it somehow in a town called Manchester, further north in Carroll County, some kind of interest-only loan. Brown sold the place, and in June of 1920, the Dorseys swung into operation in their new home on their new farm. A couple months later, Warren came along and then Emerson and Catherine and Rosie.

Eventually Brown, probably using Ed Dorsey's money, bought Ed Mellor's store on the corner of Oklahoma and Main Street, just down the hill from the Dorsey's new home. It was a big store that had been there a long time and had a good reputation and steady customers. He called it the A.C. Brown General Merchandise Store.

Later, Brown started a bank that still exists today as the Carroll Community Bank, run by his grandson Todd Brown, only now it's a few miles up the road in Eldersburg. Still later, Brown would team up with a man named Henry Forsythe, and they would run the store on Main Street together.

While Brown built his business downtown, Ed continued at Springfield until 1922. He got angry often and quit. They'd beg him to come back; he'd go back then quit again. One morning Carrie found him sitting on the side of the bed at 5 a.m.

She said, "Ed, aren't you supposed to be at work?"

"Yeah."

"Aren't you going to work?"

"No."

"Do they know you're not coming?"

"No."

"Well what's wrong?"

"I quit."

"Did you tell them?"

"Nope."

He'd stay out a while. He'd work repair crews on the B&O, sometimes near Sykesville, sometimes Baltimore. There were three passenger trains in the morning and three in the afternoon that took him wherever he needed. Once while working near Baltimore, he dropped his tools and walked off down the track without a word.

The boss was white and shouted, "Hey Ed, where you going?"

Ed said, "I'm going home."

"You're going home? Well how do I carry you on my book here? How should I list you if you're going home?"

Ed hollered back, "Fired, quit, furloughed, don't make no difference." And kept on walking.

He'd return to Springfield and quit again. Then something else came along.

In 1900, shortly after Springfield opened, only pneumonia and flu killed more Americans than tuberculosis. Usually it spreads through the air when someone coughs or sneezes. Most often it settles in the lungs, and those afflicted slowly waste away, eventually weakening, suffering terrible chest pains, and finally coughing up blood and then dying.

Because patients at Springfield lived in close quarters in large wards, TB could spread easily, even during conversations, and so in 1915, Springfield built two new cottages to isolate tuberculosis patients, one for women and one for men, but these were restricted to mentally ill white people.

The disease was much worse among the state's black population, who lived in more crowded, filthy conditions, ate poorly, and received bad medical care. Or none. By the 1920s, TB was four times higher among blacks and so bad in one section of Baltimore's black slums that they referred to it as "the lung block."

In 1922, the Maryland Board of Mental Hygiene authorized the building of the Henryton Tuberculosis Sanatorium near Isaac Anderson's old town of Marriottsville to house black tuberculosis patients.

And they hired Ed to serve as head cook and set up food service operations. Ed rode back and forth by train the four miles between Sykesville and Henryton, 10 cents each way, and worked in a place where many arrived sick and left dead, and where, according to Ed, when someone died or neared death, the turkey buzzards perched in big packs in nearby trees and roofs all around the campus.

Ed worked there two years. Then a new white supervisor came in, and Ed didn't like how he treated his black workers. And so he walked again. Back to the railroad. He landed a cooking job with the wrecking crews that cleaned up after trains crashed or derailed. They spent most of their time lounging about on wreck derricks mounted on train cars in the rail yards of Baltimore.

It was a plush job. He quit that, too. There were other small jobs here and there, but in the end, after the 12 years or so at Springfield and Henryton, and then on and off work with the B&O, Ed eventually gave up working altogether, and retired to the seclusion of his bedroom on the farm, where he would spend many years mostly alone.

Jim Crow

By 1920 when Warren was born, blacks in America were second-class citizens, except down South, where they were less. In 1865, the Thirteenth Amendment to the Constitution put an end to some 200 years of black slavery. Three years later, the Fourteenth Amendment declared that all people born in the United States, including African Americans, are full citizens of the United States. It prohibited states from passing laws restricting or harming those rights.

And finally, the Fifteenth Amendment in 1870 made it illegal to prevent people from voting based on race or color or whether they'd once been slaves. (Although this particular amendment applied to males only.) The country had begun to right its wrongs and finally realize its professed ideals.

Except it wouldn't.

After emancipation and the war, with Union troops on Southern soil, conditions for the former slaves improved, but once the soldiers left in the later 1870s, the states of the former Confederacy moved quickly to reestablish the racial order.

In *The Warmth of Other Suns*, her highly acclaimed book on the massive migration of Southern blacks to the North in the first half of the twentieth century, Pulitzer Prize–winning author Isabel Wilkerson describes what happened:

"Nursing the wounds of defeat and seeking a scapegoat, much like Germany in the years leading up to Nazism, they began to undo the opportunities accorded freed slaves during Reconstruction and to refine the language of white supremacy. They would create a caste system based not on pedigree and title, as in Europe, but solely on race, and which, by law, disallowed any movement of the lowest caste into the mainstream."

Republican influence in the South waned. Racist Democrats took control. The federal government lost interest and power, and at every opportunity, the states of the South replaced their old slave codes with a new form of subjugation based on a set of laws both written and unwritten. Collectively, these laws became known as Jim Crow.

Then a black man named Homer Plessy bought a first-class train ticket on the East Louisiana Railroad. He sat in the car reserved for whites and soon was in court and eventually the Supreme Court. It led to the famous *Plessy v. Ferguson* decision and the seven to one ruling in 1896 that if things were equal, keeping them separate was fine.

Wilkerson writes: "With a new century approaching, blacks in the South, accustomed to the liberties established after the war, were hurled back in time, as if the preceding three decades, limited though they may have been, had never happened. One by one, each license or freedom accorded them was stripped away.

"The world got smaller, narrower, more confined with each new court ruling and ordinance. Not unlike European Jews who watched the world close in on them slowly, perhaps barely perceptibly, at the start of Nazism, colored people in the South would first react in denial and disbelief to the rising hysteria, then, helpless to stop it, attempt a belated resistance, not knowing and not able to imagine how far the supremacists would go."

By the turn of the nineteenth century, and well into the twentieth, in the South, blacks were beaten, lynched, burned, and driven out of whole counties. They were hated with a passion passed down from parents to children and children to grandchildren.

But whereas the Germans set out to exterminate the Jews, the South set out merely to subjugate, humiliate, and control their former slaves. They didn't want them voting. They did want them working, for low wages, and spending some of those low wages in white-owned stores where they shopped by the thousands. They needed them and they despised them.

And as Wilkerson writes:

"Politicians began riding these anti-black sentiments all the way to governors' mansions throughout the South and to seats in the U.S. Senate. 'If it is necessary, every Negro in the state will be lynched,' James K. Vardaman, the white supremacy candidate in the 1903 Mississippi governor's race, declared."

And sure enough, first they made Vardaman governor of Mississippi, and then a U.S. Senator.

But there were worse things than electing bigots. There were the things the elected bigots allowed or condoned or cared not to see or even encouraged with their words and their actions and their laws or lack thereof.

As Wilkerson writes: "Fifteen thousand men, women, and children gathered to watch eighteen-year-old Jesse Washington as he was burned alive in Waco, Texas, in May 1916. The crowd chanted, 'Burn, burn, burn!' as Washington was lowered into the flames. One father holding his son on his shoulders wanted to make sure his toddler saw it. 'My son can't learn too young,' the father said."

Plessy v. Ferguson didn't condone or legalize violence, but it further isolated the South from the rest of the country and gave a mostly disinterested federal government even less motivation to interfere in Southern affairs. Soon Southern states put in place whatever clever Jim Crow laws they could come up with to strip blacks of their rights, disenfranchise them, subjugate them, and force them to live in fear.

In his 2010 book, *Joe Louis, Hard Times Man*, Randy Roberts sums it all up:

"Race was the soul of southern culture, and the Jim Crow laws that institutionalized the separation of blacks and whites were the constant, daily, humiliating reminders of the white belief that blacks were inferior. Jim Crow ruled virtually every area of life."

He writes of segregated railroad cars, of segregated train stations and streetcars and steamboats, of segregated hotels and water fountains and restrooms in the world where Joe Louis grew up. He writes of Jim Crow sections in "movie houses and theaters, Jim Crow entrances and exits, Jim Crow stairways and windows, Jim Crow hospitals and prisons, Jim Crow orphanages and mental facilities, and Jim Crow parks and circuses." And of course, Jim Crow schools.

He writes of "unwritten codes" that "filled in the spaces not covered by the law" and that "whether in a home or on a street, in a cotton field or at a drinking fountain, the message of the codes was the same: blacks might live in close proximity to whites, but they should have no doubts about the 'natural order of things.'

"The legal fiats of the legislators and the unwritten codes of a closed society were strictly enforced by legal and, increasingly, extralegal efforts. Students of southern history and culture observed, the litmus test of a true southerner was belief that the South should 'remain a white man's country.' Jim Crow laws provided the framework for the notion. The Ku Klux Klan and other similar white supremacist organizations contributed additional, direct muscle for enforcement."

Miss Margaret and Aunt Carrie

Warren says Sykesville was just as bad as any Jim Crow southern town, but Warren never lived in a true Jim Crow southern town, and it seems that although there was certainly racism in Sykesville and the surrounding county, it was far more benign than in the true Jim Crow American

South and, at least in some circles in Sykesville, tempered with a bit of kindness.

The *Herald* was a weak and boring paper, heavy on detail but devoid of depth, that seldom got anywhere near the bottom of a story. But it did radiate a certain stern Christian decency and did not exhibit any sort of pronounced hatred toward black people. It did not attempt to demonize them, or raise animosity against them.

In the December 20, 1917, issue, three years before Warren was born, the following appeared:

"If you want to contribute a dollar for a poor colored family, in no way to blame for their poverty, send it to *The Herald*, and we will see that it is expended for food or coal. Both are badly needed."

A week later came this.

"The poor colored family with three children mentioned to the *Herald* last week as being without food or fuel, are no longer in want, thanks to the generous response of *Herald* readers to the appeal for aid.

"Money enough was subscribed to provide coal, and contributions of provisions, clothing, etc., were sent in. The children are warmly clad, there is food in the cupboard and coal in the bin.

"The response came quickly so that the Christmas of the poor little family was a glad one after all...All that is ever necessary in Sykesville is to call attention to the needs of anyone in distress to bring the needed relief."

And yet, in the May 3, 1917, issue, just a few months earlier, the *Herald* carried an article about the town's main entertainment venue under the headline, "Minstrel Makes a Hit."

"The Lyceum was crowded to the doors on last Thursday night to witness the minstrel performance given by the Washington Stock Company, composed of some very talented and professional black face artists. The performance was held for the benefit of St. Joseph's Catholic Church of this place...Father Cainan is to be congratulated on bringing such an array of talent to Sykesville and hopes to have similar treats in the future."

That "black face artists" might be considered insulting to the town's small black population seems not to have occurred to the *Herald* or Father Cainan or the people of Sykesville who packed the town's theater to watch white men with black-painted faces imitate real black people in most likely unflattering ways.

Regardless of how the town might have viewed and treated its black residents when Warren was a boy, or how its attitudes toward those residents evolved over time, Main Street Sykesville in the teens and twenties and Main Street Sykesville in the thirties were two different places. Up till at least 1927, Wade Warfield dominated, and there was a sense the town was thriving, growing, and just starting to realize its potential.

Warfield had his store, well-stocked, well-run, and profitable. Out back, his milling and supply company and coal and lumber businesses boomed. They were still building at Springfield, and the trains brought in his lumber and coal.

In 1917 for $5000, Warfield sold land to B.F. Shriver & Company, a big canning operation out of Westminster. Shriver built a large canning complex just over the river as you left town.

They canned peas, tomatoes, vegetables, and sweet corn, and in the twenties and into the thirties, Main Street Sykesville was a busy place, as farmers came from all over the area, lining up with their wagons and carts to unload at the canning factory or at Maryland Milling and Supply, where they would drop off wheat and pick up feed and equipment and supplies.

In the twenties, with the trains coming in and the canning factory in full operation and Warfield's business booming and farms all around, with the farmers unloading and the hospital across the way building, the town was busy, crowded, and full of horses and wagons and mules and the sounds and smells of a thriving agricultural mecca, an oasis of commerce in the middle of endless fields of green.

But soon the fall of Warfield, followed by the Depression, a massive fire on Main Street, and the war, ended any notion that Sykesville would become a thriving metropolis in the farmland, and ushered in an era of perpetual poverty, of just getting by, of slowly falling apart, of eventually losing its self-sufficiency.

Warfield's fire in 1920 was more than a harbinger of his own doom; it was a prelude to Sykesville's long slide toward becoming a riverside ghost town with a polluted river and abandoned Main Street.

There's a book called *Images of America, Sykesville* by Bill Hall. The book is part of a series about American places. It's mostly pictures. The cover has a brown and yellow tint intended to suggest old time photographs. On the cover is a man on a lawn in a rocker with a big hat, a big moustache, and a rope attached to a big horse. His name is John Harris. The book says Harris was a harness maker who died in 1926 and founded the Harris Grocery store in 1901.

Harris had several sons and a couple daughters, and the store he founded on Main Street would become a Sykesville institution. On page 84 of Hall's book, there are two pictures of a woman named Margaret Harris. In one, she's young and wearing a nice coat and ridiculously large hat that shades her face, and above that there's another from 1950. Margaret is older in that one, gray haired and stocky, with glasses, a plain dress, a bit of a smile, and just five years short of an early death.

By 1950, all the Dorsey children except one had moved away, but in the twenties and thirties, Margaret Harris was a key ally in Carrie Dorsey's battle for survival. What started as a grocery store became an all-purpose shopping place, a grocery store, a department store, and a place where, for reasons Warren doesn't understand, Carrie Dorsey was able to work a bit of magic to help keep her family fed and clothed.

"Margaret Harris was around my mother's age," Warren says. "She was in her thirties, and every year, my mother used to take us to Margaret Harris, who operated the dry goods side of the business, and Margaret Harris would fit all of us with shoes. We all went at once and lined up, and she gave us shoes. And as far as I know, my mother never fully paid for anything she got. She paid a dollar here, a dollar there.

"I never understood the relationship, but when she went to the Harris store she never had any trouble getting what she needed. I don't think the bill was ever settled, and I don't think Marion or Margaret Harris ever badgered her because of a bill.

"I have a little book my mother used to keep expenditures in. Every now and then it has an entry. Sometimes it says 'Margaret,' and other times it says 'Harris.' A dollar, or sometimes two dollars, so whenever she got a dollar or two she could spare she would pay on the bill.

"Carrie never came away from Marion Harris without groceries. He wasn't particularly friendly, and neither was Margaret Harris, but they weren't unfriendly, either.

"There were no 'whites only' signs around town. You could go into any store in Sykesville, I think. You just had to know your place. We had to call her 'Miss Margaret.' They would always call my mother 'Aunt Carrie,' which I guess was a little less than calling her Mrs., or recognizing her on an equal status.

"The store was divided. One side operated by Marion Harris was strictly groceries, and you would go through a little areaway to the dry goods side, where Margaret operated. She sold clothes. She sold material for sewing. A lot of people sewed in those days."

Warren's oldest brother, Clifton, drove a delivery truck for the Harrises part-time. Margaret Harris frequently gathered up used clothes and let Carrie sort through them for anything useful.

Later, she helped get several Dorsey boys into the Roosevelt administration's Civilian Conservation Corp. But yet the women were not friends, could not be friends, and their interaction always took place strictly within the confines of the Harris store, Margaret calling Carrie "Aunt Carrie," and Carrie calling Margaret "Miss Margaret."

Better Days Coming

The farmhouse they bought from A.C. Brown was hardly luxurious. Ed scrounged what furniture he could. There were beds in the bedrooms and a table in the kitchen and a hodge-podge of furniture throughout. The living room sat unused, except for Christmas and thunderstorms.

When it thundered, Carrie herded all the kids into the living room.

"During thunderstorms everything stopped," Warren says. "And we gathered in the living room and sat in the dark in silence until the storm was over, because Carrie said, 'That's the good Lord speaking.'"

The kids called her "Carrie." They called their father "Ed." They spent much of their time gathered in the kitchen, especially in cold weather. The kitchen had heat from the stove, and that was the only heat in the house.

They used kerosene lamps until they got electricity in 1930, several years after the white part of town. Water came from their well or their stream and wasn't purified in any way. Milk came straight from the cow. The place was dark, dusty, bug infested, and noisy. It smelled of farm animals. The railroad was just down the hill, and the engines roared down the tracks morning, noon, and night, blowing their whistles, rattling empty westward, then back eastward, cars rumbling and wheels squealing, bringing huge loads of coal from the mines in Western Maryland and West Virginia toward the docks in Baltimore, 100 cars at a time, or more, two separate train lines weaving along the river, and all day long the noise of passenger trains and coal cars, a never ending rattle and squeal and roar, the constant warning whistles as the train crossed the intersection by the road out of town.

They had several animals and put them to good use. There was a horse and a cow. There were hunting dogs and chickens and pigs.

Warren says, "At one time we had our own sow and produced our own young pigs, but at other times we had to bargain with farmers to buy piglets. We'd feed them through the summer, and toward the end, we started feeding them mostly corn to get them as fat as we could, because the fatter they are, the more lard you can harvest. Usually in November, after the weather turned cold, we did the butchering.

"My daddy was very good at that, and after the butchering, we cured the meat with salt and smoked it and put it in a big barrel, and layers of salt and layers of meat that he cut up, and let it stay there a couple of weeks and hung it up, and it would be okay to eat. So that was our meat for the winter.

"And for lard, which is hog fat, you take the fat meat and separate it from the rest of the meat and put it in a big pot and heat it and cook it till it's very well done and then we used a lard press, a hand gadget you poured it in and pressed the oil out.

"And if you left the lard to cool, it would be semi-solid. You put that in a can. The Harrises bought lard in 50-pound cans and when they were empty they gave the cans away, so we had these big cans, and we used the lard for frying food and making bread. My mother made all the bread. Occasionally, if she had a little extra money, she baked a pie or something and used the lard to make the crust."

Ed even used the animals to pay the mortgage. The interest on the loan was $40 a year. A key component of self-sufficiency was producing milk. To do that, they needed a cow, but at a certain point cows stop producing, unless, as Warren puts it, "They're serviced by a bull."

So Ed would have his cow serviced each year by another farmer's bull, and each year the cow would have a calf and Ed would use the calf to pay the mortgage. He didn't show up at the bank and shove a small cow through the teller's window. He sold the calf and used the money to satisfy the bank.

Ed had his vision. Raise his own food, pick berries, grow crops, milk the cow, raise chickens for eggs and food and trading, use water from their well and stream, cut wood for the stove, slaughter pigs for meat, and supplement that by hunting rabbits and squirrels.

"We had three hunting dogs that were as much a part of the family as anything, Old Bess, Old Jack, and Old Sport," Warren says. "They were mixed breed, but mostly beagle. They hunted on farms all around our area.

"We had several 12-gauge shot guns. Devries in Sykesville used to sell shells. They sold guns, too. My father had his pet gun. He had a pump gun that would hold six shells in the magazine, which means you could put one in the muzzle. That means he could start out with the ability to fire up to seven times in rapid succession.

"We used to hunt rabbits. We used to hunt squirrels. The only kind of meat we ordinarily had was pork meat, which was salt cured, but come rabbit season, my daddy and the older boys, sometimes they'd come back with 12 to 20 rabbits. That was an important source of fresh meat.

"Squirrels weren't as plentiful, and of course, there isn't a whole lot on a squirrel, but my mother used to make a stew out of them."

There were no deer, at least none he remembers, and if there had been, they would certainly have killed and eaten them and maybe even thrived on them.

He says, "Any animal that was catchable was edible."

The main point was to go to the white people for nothing. But running the farm was hard and constant labor, and despite Ed's skills and resourcefulness and creative mind, and because of something dark and mysterious in his personality, most of the work of running the farm and feeding and raising the kids, eventually fell on Carrie.

"The one constant in our family was my mother," Warren says. "She was the engine that drove the Dorsey Machine. And she was determined this would be done with the least impact on our future.

"Instead of rebelling against the segregated society, or reacting to the insulting ways we were treated, she found if she could accept this as the dilemma she had to work through to raise us, she could work through this maze of denial of services and denial of opportunity, and that's what she did.

"She did this with what I would call 'mother wit,' skills she learned growing up, skills she learned from Aunt Kitty."

The family always needed money. For oil for lamps. For sugar and grain and meal and flour. For feed for the animals. For clothes, or at least the materials and tools to patch up clothes.

So Carrie did laundry for white people. During summer, she coordinated the kids as they worked together on the farm to grow and gather and harvest and sell.

Warren says, "Everybody had a hand in raising food. During the summer it was a full-time job. We used to put out 200 tomato plants. That's a lot of tomatoes, and Carrie used to can them herself.

"It was an everyday thing to be out in the garden. If it wasn't one thing, it was another. Weeds were always a nuisance. Every day, everybody had a hand in doing the weeds.

"And potato bugs were a constant problem. The bugs grow on the potato vines. The larvae can ravage the vines if you don't get them off, and you won't have any potatoes if you don't have any vines. So you take a stick and go along pushing the bugs into a bucket.

"My brother Emerson was always joking. He claimed he was born in the morning and by afternoon they had him out in the garden bugging potatoes.

"You had to worry about getting the bugs off the beans too. You could do it chemically if you had the money to buy the chemicals. It was better what we did, health wise."

It was long, hot, tiring work, mostly done by children.

Warren says, "We couldn't afford the alternative to not doing it. It was just a way of life, and you just accepted it without questioning it. At the end of the day you're tired, I'll tell you."

They kept what they needed and sold the rest if they could. Or traded it.

"Peddlers, stores, any place, there was always someone who would buy stuff," Warren says. "That was a vital pipeline of cash."

So they worked and saved and scraped and planned. Margaret Harris helped them. And Carrie said the same thing all the time. "There's a better day a-coming. There are better days than this for you."

But not for her. Carrie understood her situation. She had no time for resentment, and no practical means of rebelling. There were animals to care for, crops to plant and grow and harvest, potato vines to bug, mouths to feed, babies to watch, and usually another on the way. Between 1904 and 1926 she had 12 children without losing one.

She had very little money and quite a few needs. She kept her small notebooks with month-by-month expenditures. I'm looking at one now. It's four inches wide by six inches long. The outside cover is hard and brown and slightly torn. Inside, there's dark print, a black rectangle and inside the rectangle, the words "The Baltimore & Ohio Railroad Company," fresh like they were printed yesterday.

The hard inside covers are white and filled with figures in pencil, running up and down and sideways, numbers crossed out, calculations crossed out, lots of sums correctly added, a long string of random tied-together zeroes that seem to serve no purpose at all, as if she's practicing her zeroes, or fell asleep drawing circles, or is trying to make some point.

But inside, it becomes orderly. The first page of entries is February 1933. The paper has yellowed. There are blue lines with a hint of green, Carrie's neat handwriting between the lines, Carrie's invisible fingerprints, maybe flakes of Carrie's skin, the penciled imprint of her thoughts and worries, scraped into yellowed pages, brown and curled and crumbling at their edges.

There are missing pages and the page for February barely clings to the book. I'm staring at the scrawlings, scrutinizing the calculations made by a slave's daughter in 1933, a woman in her forties, a mind at work 80 years ago working out the basics of survival.

When Carrie scrawled these numbers and added them up, the country was in the heart of the Great Depression, Adolph Hitler was tightening his grip on power, and war was coming. But that was still a few years off, and she had no way of knowing that soon, Thelma's husband, Mae's husband, and three of her boys would be called into service, or that one day one of her son's wives would run to her home crying, clutching a telegram with bad news. Right now she was worried about corn and stockings and chickenmash.

February, 1933

Corn 1.00
insurence 2.00
Chester .50
Chickenmash 1.28
insurence 3.25
papers .50
stockings .40
union suit .35
Miss Harris 1.00
corn 2.00
dishpan .75
skillet .15
brick .10
insurence 1.00
union suit .35
lodge 1.30
cough syrup .25
corn syrup .25
bismuth 1.00

She kept small life insurance policies on each of her children. Warren believes they paid out $25. A union suit was an undergarment, and she bought those for Ed. They were one-piece outfits, and the kids never got union suits, they got feed bags.

And the cough syrup was probably called Juniper Tar. Warren never saw it spelled and remembers a slightly different pronunciation, but you can find something on the Internet called Juniper Tar that sounds just like the stuff he remembers.

He says, "It came in a little bottle of dark fluid. It was some kind of extract of tar, and you poured this tar-like stuff on a spoonful of sugar and we would swallow it, and it was supposed to be good for colds.

"I remember the bottle. They had one guy who looked nice and healthy and another one who didn't look so healthy. And the healthy one said, 'I drink Juniper Tar.' And the other one said, 'I don't.'"

The total expenditures for February of 1933 were $17.43. For March, $21.51, including 75 cents for pulling a tooth, another dollar for Miss Harris, 35 cents for a broom, and $4.25 for "things from Wards."

In April and May, there were $1 fees under doctor. In May, there's $6.50 for pigs and $1.35 for hog powder. In July, $1 to Dr. Sprecher, 15 cents for bloomers, $2 for fertilizer, $2.25 for Pain King, $1.10 for cement, $10 to Thelma, and 14 cents for Black Flag.

And in July, there was a very odd expenditure, $5 for a pool table.

Warren explains that one. "My daddy converted the stable into a poolroom. He got two pool tables from Barnes, who had the whites-only pool hall on Main Street. I think they were something Barnes was discarding, and Ed put them in the stable, and people from around the community would come and shoot pool.

"He charged five cents a game. He was really good. Nobody who came to his pool hall was any competition for him."

After buying the pool table, Carrie went back to necessities or more mundane expenditures. In September, she bought a cow for $25. In October, she paid $2.89 for electric. In November, $6 for coal. In December, not a single mention of Christmas, but the bill was $69.93 and mentions $20 for Chester and $17 for Vernon.

In February of 1934, she bought limewater, worm tablets, a mop handle, and spent 25 cents on toothbrushes. In September 1936, $17 for glasses.

Usually the monthly bill was in the twenties, sometimes the thirties, and often in the forties, but seldom more than that.

Ed worked sometimes, but mostly, over time, he became more hidden. He stayed in his room, hardly spoke to the kids, seldom ate with them, seldom even came downstairs, not even during thunderstorms to heed the voice of the Lord.

So it all fell to Carrie. Her name was appropriate. Carrie. For the first 10 years on the farm, she had no electricity. She had no washer or dryer or running water, no health care and no heat. She carried the family with what she had.

Carrie's Week

And every week, it went pretty much the same way. On Mondays she set up three washtubs on a long wooden bench on the back porch just outside the kitchen, except in winter, when she set up in the kitchen. The tubs were big tin things, maybe three feet in diameter.

In the first, she'd hand wash everything with a washboard and big yellow bar of some sort of borax soap. First she'd rub on the soap. Then she'd rub the clothes on the washboard to scrub off as much dirt as she could. Next she'd boil the clothes on the cookstove to wash away suds and loosen up what the scrubbing missed.

She didn't have any of what we refer to today as appliances. She had the cookstove. She used the stove for laundry. She used it to cook and heat the house. It warmed the water for baths, which the kids took in the kitchen in the same big tubs their mom used to wash clothes. They took turns getting in the tub, shared the same water, boys in one shift, girls in another. They each got one bath a week.

After boiling the clothes, Carrie put the clothes in a second rinse, whites first, then the work clothes, where she tried to get out as much dirt and suds as possible. And finally it went into a third tub with bluing in it to brighten the colors and get rid of all traces of soap.

Tuesday

The dryer was a bunch of clotheslines strung from tree to tree in the backyard on Tuesdays. This worked fairly well, except in winter when the clothes froze and she'd bring them inside and find places to dry them in the cold house, then iron them with a flat iron heated on the cookstove. She'd set up the ironing board in the kitchen near the stove and get started after breakfast, first doing the clothes she took in for white women.

When Warren left in 1937, Carrie still did laundry for Mrs. Rocker who lived on the hill in back of Main Street.

"And we'd go down and get the clothes and after they'd been laundered, we had to take them back," he remembers. "And my mother got all of 50 cents a week to do the laundry. It was a good amount for the family in those days."

With the white people's clothes out of the way, she could turn to the tough job of her own family's clothes, all the while, as she ironed, pulling things out for patching and buttons and other repairs.

She ironed all day, with stops to fix meals, feed animals, and get the kids off to school. She'd had Clifton at 19, and Warren, the ninth, at 34. When Warren was five, she also had nine-year-old Vernon, seven-year old Chester, six-year-old Mae, three-year old Emerson, one-year old Catherine, and Rosie on the way.

Wednesday

On Wednesdays she sewed. She replaced buttons, patched up holes, improvised underwear.

Warren says, "My mother had a treadle sewing machine, and she was pretty adept at doing it. And she was able to make or adapt our clothes mostly. I never had a store-bought suit until I was, I think the first suit I ever had, I was in college. I always had hand-me-downs.

"We never had more than about two changes of underwear. I never had store-bought underwear as long as I lived at home. She made our underwear, usually out of feed bags. The feed used to come in a sort of muslin material. Some had print and some had none, and a lot of people used to make clothes from the bags."

The rest were hand-me-downs or stuff Margaret Harris collected. Dressing the kids was a big improvising, mending, and salvaging operation, and pretty much filled every Wednesday.

Also on Wednesdays, schedule permitting, there was another operation. They needed fuel for the stove. One source was coal. As the endless coal hoppers rumbled by toward Baltimore, coal flew off and bounced and rolled and stopped in the ground and the grass, and Carrie and the older kids would sack it up and carry it back to the house.

"My mother could put a sack of coal on her back, which must have weighed 100 pounds, and carry it that whole distance, which must have been half a mile."

Thursday

The floors were bare wood, with linoleum in the kitchen, and on Thursdays, she swept and scrubbed every floor. Also on Thursdays, they cleared the house, whitewashed the walls, and battled flies. There were no screens, and it got hot, and they opened the windows, and the flies poured in.

"There were flies everywhere, because there were all kinds of breeding places," Warren says. "We had animals. We had outhouses.

"Flour came in paper sacks, and we would cut it, and strip it, and tie the strips around a pole, and try to shoo flies out. Beyond that, you could buy Black Flag Insect Powder. She'd put it on a flat piece of paper or a bowl, and she'd blow it by mouth, to aerosolize it. Then go out of the house for a half hour, at least, and then you'd go back in and sweep up the flies. You could get dustpans full."

A week later, the flies were back.

Also on Thursdays, she took care of the beds. Bed bugs were a constant problem, and most days Warren woke up thoroughly bitten. To discourage the bugs, Carrie took the beds apart, took them out into the yard, and sprayed them with gasoline from a hand sprayer. She'd hit the cracks and crevices and springs.

Each year they got a new mattress made of ticking stuffed with straw. They spilled out the straw mashed by a year's sleeping and filled it again. And the bed smelled like gasoline, and Warren shared it with Emerson and Chester and lots of small blood-sucking insects.

In summer, they sweated terribly all night or opened the windows and sweated less, but now the mosquitoes came in with the smell of farm, the roar of trains, and countless other sorts of insects, along with flies by the hundreds.

In winter, they shivered. There was no heat. There was no insulation in the walls. A glass of water would freeze overnight in their bedroom. They buried themselves under blankets and got warm till morning where they could see their breath in the gas lamp in the freezing cold while they dressed for school.

Friday

Fridays depended and changed with the seasons. In summer they roamed far and wide picking fruits and wild berries that Carrie made into jelly and preserves. And of course, every day in summer there was the weeding and the bugging and all the other hard work of managing a small family farm.

Saturday

On Saturday Carrie put a basket over her arm and took one of the kids downtown, where it would be crowded, and she'd visit the Harris store for meal and sugar, and Margaret's side, where she might pick up needles and thread and whatever else she could to keep the family clothed.

Sunday

Sunday was mostly for rest, except that they had to make sure they had enough water for the next day's washing. That meant filling tubs and lard cans and pots and whatever else they could from the well beside the house, or in summer when the well went dry, from the stream that ran across their property.

Ed never went to church and probably wouldn't have believed much he heard there. Carrie went, but not often. The kids always went, and then in summer after church, to a local ball game, and sometimes Carrie would play hide and seek with them, only not very well.

As Warren puts it, "By the time I came along, Carrie had expanded in girth, and she used to hide behind the tree as if she thought she was concealed, but we still went through the charade of looking for her.

"But the rest of the week, she stuck to her schedule. It wasn't absolutely rigid, but it was a general schedule she followed, and even though this was a simple woman with little education, she was able to organize and come up with resources that took a lot of ingenuity.

"And most of the time she was doing all that work, she was pregnant. In 22 years, all the children were born. She raised her babies from breast milk, and soon as we were weaned from breast milk, we were raised on raw cow's milk. I hear you have various formulas now, but we didn't have any formula.

"And when we were weaned off milk to solid food, she would chew the food and then transfer it to her children.

"My mother was always the stabilizing force. She made sure we were cared for in spite of all the odds against her. She was able to work with people who otherwise were hostile toward the African-American community. But for whatever reasons, they helped her. She found a way to get things done.

"Life wasn't easy for anyone in those days, but it was particularly difficult for people of color."

The Sykesville Giants

As tough as all that sounds, the other people on Oklahoma Hill thought the Dorseys were rich. The Dorseys were the aristocracy, the landed gentry. The Dorseys were somehow different, more educated, an upper class among the lowest class, and everyone addressed Carrie and Ed with respect.

The neighborhood was mostly a row of beat-up houses along a ridge. The first house at the bottom of the hill, not far from the train station and just across from Warfield's burned mill, belonged to Dr. Sprecher, the town doctor, who unlike most doctors in those days, treated blacks and whites equally, opened his doors to all, and delivered the last of Carrie's children. After the doctor's house, came the Chipleys, another white family.

Both the doctor's house and the Chipley's were among the original summer cottages built by Frank Brown. The Chipley's house is still there, beautifully renovated by Jonathan Herman, but of Sprecher's house, only the front steps, a twisted railing, and some stone foundation remain.

After that, further up Oklahoma, on the left side of the road, came Hepner's shacks, where the black people lived. The hill overlooked a steeply climbing road out front and descended rapidly toward the river and the railroad tracks out back.

In all, there were 14 black families up there, and some quite large. Warren's oldest brother, Clifton, settled up there and added another 12 Dorsey children, the oldest barely younger than Warren. Vernon and Everett also settled up there. Vernon had four daughters. Everett added five kids. There were 18 Johnsons, if you include the parents.

Few of the men had good or permanent jobs. Ed cooked at Springfield until he didn't anymore. Hagen Bond drove a truck for Maryland Milling and Supply. Jack Johnson, the father of 16, worked in the fertilizer factory at the bottom of the hill, where fertilizer arrived in boxcars, and they mixed it to a farmer's specifications.

"Jack was the chief person in charge," Warren says. "He used to come out of there at the end of the day covered in the dust, and they didn't have any masks or anything of that sort, and he had to breathe that stuff all day."

Most everyone struggled along, doing odd jobs, day work on farms, cleaning up around stores. They were often hungry, cold in winter, afflicted with flies and mosquitos and bedbugs in the humid Maryland summers, as well as the constant squeal of the trains and grinding drain of persistent worry. There wasn't much to look forward to or be terribly proud of.

There was their small cold school. There was St. Luke's, their small cold church across the way. And there was a baseball team called the Sykesville Giants. And that was the best thing they had, and the source of some of Warren's most fond memories.

He says, "At that time, baseball was a universal pastime in every black enclave that could gather enough young men. Anywhere you'd go, any African-American community, if they had enough young men, they had a team."

Sykesville was no exception. In fact, Sykesville was exceptional. The team organized around 1915. Each player bought his own glove and uniform. They carved a field from woodland and a couple farms that bordered the community. Nobody seemed to own the land. It was undeveloped, and before long it was a baseball field and a place for picnics and reunions and parties, and the main attraction was usually a Giants game.

By the time Warren grew up, the Giants were the best team around, and black teams traveled from miles to challenge them. They had hitting, fielding, and a great pitcher, a first cousin of Ed's, known to Warren only as Cousin Clendan.

Warren says, "Clendan had mastered a sharp breaking pitch that seemed to say, now you see me, now you don't. He called it Old Henry. Today it's called the slider. Cousin Clendan could throw a slider before there even was a slider."

When Clendan pitched, he would go nine innings and the Giants would win, but he wasn't always on the mound, because he had a problem with what Warren refers to as "the consumption of spirits."

He says, "If you caught him when he was in the spirits, he couldn't pitch. But when Clendan wasn't in the spirits he was invincible. He pitched to a man named Gene Norris, who was a tremendously good catcher, and Gene kept up a constant chatter, and any time he'd say, 'this batter has a notion,' that was a signal to Clendan. Time for Old Henry. The result was usually a swinging strike-out or a weak grounder to the infield."

The catcher's dad was also on the team. They called him "the old dude at third." He was about 40. His name was James Norris, but the kids called him "Mr. Jim," and he was sort of the team father. He was also the guy who kept their church running. He paid the bills and raised funds from the white community, where sometimes he worked as a handyman.

Mainly, he worked as the groundskeeper on the Brooks property, a mansion down near the Patapsco on the other side of the river, where Mr. Jim lived in a tenant house.

He was also the gravedigger at the Springfield Presbyterian Church where most of the white people were buried. He and his boys, Gene and Earl, dug all the graves by hand and most likely dug Wade Warfield's in 1935.

There's a street in town called Norris Avenue where mostly white people live today, and where certainly none of them realize their street is named for a black third baseman who dug graves with his boys.

Warren's brother Russell played shortstop.

"Russell was an excellent player," Warren says. "He was only about five-feet-four and 135 pounds, but he made up for his size with tremendous skill and passion. He loved baseball. His wife said even to his dying days, Russell talked about the glory of playing shortstop for the Sykesville Giants.

"Russell was 11 years older than I am. During the week, he was a laborer in the maintenance gang for the B&O, very demanding work. It was a real challenge to get up to play on the weekend. But Russell was always ready."

Aside from Clendan, the team's superstar was their towering cleanup hitter, first baseman Raymond Lewis, who everyone called Big Raymond. Big Raymond's brother Kick Lewis played second, and Warren never knew him by any name other than Kick.

He says, "Almost everyone had a nickname. Often we didn't know the real names of people. A lot of people never knew my real name. They only knew Tom. My father used to recite a nursery rhyme. 'Little Tommy Tittlemouse lived in a little house. He caught fishes in other men's ditches.' And somehow I got stuck with that name, and it got shortened to Tom."

Speedster David Grooms played right, and Clarence Green played center. David was about the same age as Russell and worked in the same labor gang. Clarence also worked on the railroad and moved into the house the

Dorseys once lived in before A.C. Brown sold them his house and farm.

The left fielder was a guy named Roger Anderson, who spent his weeks working odd jobs, spent his spare time in pickup games with smaller kids, and also played the banjo.

"He'd gotten an old banjo from someplace," Warren says. "He probably got the inspiration from his daddy, Mr. Wes Anderson, who was the only man in the community who kept and trained coonhounds. Everybody else hunted mostly rabbits and birds. Mr. Wes hunted coons.

"But he also played a guitar and would sit on his front porch, and you would hear him playing on his guitar and singing all kinds of made-up stuff about life. He wasn't what you'd consider a skilled musician."

They got their baseballs at Devries Hardware in town, the same place they got the shells for their shotguns, and used the balls till the covers came off. If a ball went into the woods along the field, a group of boys swarmed into the underbrush and tracked it down.

But the days of the Giants were short-lived. By the thirties, most of the players had ventured off in search of jobs and better lives. Banjo-playing Roger Anderson died in New York City. Russell lived most of his life in Baltimore. Only Clarence Green and Gene Norris lived their whole lives on Oklahoma Hill.

It wasn't just the Depression or growing older that ruined the glory days of the Giants. First came the white guy on the horse with the spear, who charged up and down the first baseline practicing for jousting competitions.

Then came the garbage. There were always two or three grocery stores in town. And one of the stores began dumping its trash behind left field. Other businesses caught on and started dumping their trash, too, and slowly the playing field got polluted and destroyed and forgotten.

Warren says, "There was no regard for the people who lived next to the property and considered it their playing field. The standard attitude of the white community toward us, where rights and privileges were concerned, was your concerns are no concern of ours. When I left in 1937, our old field was a town dump."

The Magic of the Rocks

White kids didn't play baseball against black kids, or go to school with them, or have much of anything else to do with them. There was white Sykesville. There was black Sykesville. And there was one strange exception.

The town always had an odd relationship with the river. For the most part it was calm and shallow and not very wide, but on occasion it would flood and change the course of the town's history. At other times, it would save the town, by providing the only water available to stop a raging fire. And for many years, the river also served pretty much as the town's sewer. It was a dirty town and a dirty river.

But apparently the river did more than sometimes destroy the town, soak up its waste, and put out its fires. It also worked some sort of magic, and Warren wrote this story about it.

The Rocks— Sykesville's Improbable Enigma

In my youth, Sykesville was a location of strict racial segregation. Other than shopping in the local stores and the employer-employee encounters, there were only incidental contacts between the races. Any contact in public accommodations, religious institutions, educational establishments or social gatherings was taboo. This code of conduct was absolute with one generally known, but conveniently ignored exception, the shared use of a swimming hole – "the rocks."

About a half mile up river from the bridge that crosses the Patapsco in Sykesville, there was an expanse about 30 feet wide and 200 feet long. At the deepest end, the water measured about five feet; at the most shallow it measured about three. In my youth, about 80 to 90 years ago, this area of the river was known by locals as the rocks.

This area of the river was secluded by trees and bushes along both banks. On the north side was a huge rock that rose about five feet above water level and stretched about 20 feet along the riverbank. The surface of the boulder was nearly flat, affording an ideal place to disrobe. The customary preparation to entering the water was to strip nude, and only male youth frequented the swimming hole.

Who were these boys? One group was the white youths that lived in the main area of the town; the other was the African-American youths who lived on Oklahoma Hill. The day-to-day divide between the groups conformed to the strict segregation of Sykesville. Swimming in the rocks was the improbable exception.

The white boys reached the swimming hole by walking west from the bridge over the river along the B&O Railway—the half-mile distance to the rocks. African Americans walked down the hill bordering the B&O from the Oklahoma community. A path through the trees along the riverbank led from the railway to the rocks.

You entered the swimming hole through a narrow path through the trees that lined the banks. Both groups randomly sought out the waters of the rocks throughout the summer. At times both were present for a swim. There was never a scheduled meeting and there was never an effort to be the only group present. Mixed groups frolicking in the water without any negative encounters was the usual happening.

When the boys emerged from swimming to return to their homes, the interlude of tranquility evaporated and we returned to the racial divide of daily life. Each group found its way through the narrow strand of trees that bordered the pool back into the racial divide. Once again a brief interlude of racial harmony dissolved. The cooling respite of color blindness at the pool faded into our divided reality. The magic of the rocks was replaced by the reality of daily life.

What was the magic? Could it have been the mythical man of magic, "Merlin," working his mischief, waving his wand over the waters and transforming them into a balm of forgetfulness so that those who swam there could only see the unity of the Master's humanity?

I only know that in the reality of my youth in the days I lived on Oklahoma Hill in Sykesville, the rocks was an improbable enigma. Now as I ponder the past in the waning years of my life, I am bothered by what might have been. Did the rocks hold the secret to dissolving the destructive racial divide that plagued an otherwise perfect union that is America? Is the solution for racial harmony as simple as the magic of the rocks?

Dunk the Nigger

That magic never got far past the river. The white boys got there one way, the blacks another. There were no planned meetings, but on hot summer days, they took off their clothes and played together. They didn't fight or argue or call each other names. They splashed around and then went home the way they came and sort of forgot about one another.

There wasn't any great animosity beyond the river. There was no tension between black and white Sykesville. There were just two isolated communities, one tucked away up a hill behind the other, and very little contact between them.

Sykesville had a small volunteer fire department, and each year they held a carnival on the grounds of the school where the white kids went. The carnival was one of those rare places the town's white and black people sort of mingled. They let the black kids and their parents come to the carnival. They restricted them to certain activities and there'd be a short time each night when they let the black kids on the rides.

But the biggest attraction and the thing that sticks most in Warren's mind from 80 years ago, was a dunking booth. You've seen them. Hit a lever with a baseball and someone falls in the water. At the Sykesville carnival, it was always a black man, and there was always a long line waiting to throw a ball and knock the guy in the water, and Warren would approach the line and hear the shouting and pass the line and still hear the shouting, as he walked away. He still hears it.

"The actual name of the attraction is completely lost in my memory," he says. "All I remember is a surreal noise and all the people in line chanting, 'Dunk the nigger. Dunk the nigger. Dunk the nigger.'"

He contends they're still playing that game today. Only the nigger's not a man in a dunking booth anymore. He's a black man in a white house in Washington D.C.

The Genius Horse

By necessity and inclination, they were frugal and resourceful. Ed built his own tools. He built a pool hall in a barn and charged a nickel a game. He paid the mortgage with a calf.

Carrie traded eggs for needles and thread so she could put clothes together or make clothes out of discards and feed sacks. When the kids got sick, she treated them with Juniper Tar or Pain King. You rubbed on Pain King for sprains or burns or bruises. You swallowed it for headaches, toothaches, nausea, bad moods, depression, grippe, pimples, and just about anything else that ailed you. And if your horse had a problem, Pain King worked wonders on horses, too.

And the Dorseys had a wonderful horse. He came with the place. He'd been there longer than Warren. He was a friend, a member of the family, a four-legged key to the whole operation, and when Frank passed away, Warren cried like he lost a brother.

And like Ed, and like Warren, and so many Dorseys to come, Frank bordered on genius. At least among his species. They could travel miles with Frank pulling the wagon. When it was time to go home, no matter how far they'd gone, no matter the direction or the meandering of the path, they could let go of the reins and Frank would take them home.

And when it came to precision plowing without tearing up anything that wasn't meant to be torn up, Frank understood completely. He was an expert plow horse, eager, skilled, and strong. He knew exactly what was expected, and did it perfectly.

When he died, the older brothers were off raising families and working jobs. Warren was around 14, Emerson 12. And all the hard work fell to them. Without Frank, suddenly carrying wood from the back fields became much harder work, and so did plowing the potato crop that year. In fact, they couldn't do it.

Then Romulus showed up. Romulus was not a horse. He was one of the brothers. He was 19 and the fourth of the brothers after Clifton, and Everett, and Russell. He worked as a cook at Henryton and lived there, too, and one day he would try to make a bit of extra money moonlighting at Renehan's Apple Butter factory and accidentally feed his left hand to an apple-slicing machine that made no distinction between fingers and apples. But this was before

89

that, when Rom was young and healthy and had 10 good fingers and lots of good ideas, too.

"Rom was an innovator," Warren says. "Kitchens, especially in institutions or restaurants, they have a lot of waste oil, and they collected it in tanks, and there were people who would buy it, and Rom's old cars sometimes were using oil so much, he got the idea of using this cooking oil from Henryton for lubrication, and I guess it worked. It produced a lot of smoke, but Rom ran his cars on it."

So one day, with the potatoes ready and Frank dead and Warren and Emerson desperate, they hitched the plow to Rom's car and, with the youngest Dorsey boys on either side of the plow to guide it along, and all kinds of smoke shooting out the exhaust, they plowed up the potatoes with Romulus Dorsey's mechanical horse.

Fire on Main Street

By late summer of 1937, as the Great Depression lingered and Germany became increasingly dark and frightening, Sykesville had become small, depressed, and poor, and for the black people up Oklahoma Hill, a very hard place to make a living.

The Dorseys needed every penny, but that summer, Carrie made an exception. Up till then any money anyone in the family made went to the family, but Warren had a scholarship. Warren was accepted to Morgan College. He had a way out. And Carrie let him keep his earnings.

The best way to make money, maybe the only way for an uneducated teenage black boy in those days, was to work farms. It was common to see boys both black and white out working the fields all around the town. Slaves were no longer an option, but young kids were cheap. They thinned corn. They pulled peas from pea vines. They cleaned what they called field greens from wheat fields and cornfields to prepare for harvest.

That final summer, and the summer before, Warren followed threshing machines from farm to farm all over southern Carroll and northern Howard County for 15 cents an hour.

He says, "When I was a youngster, farmers didn't have machines that would cut the wheat and thresh it out. They cut the wheat, and the machine would tie it into bundles. Then people like me would go and stack it in the fields. You'd have all these shucks of wheat all in the field.

"Then a man who owned two threshing machines would go from farm to farm and thresh out the grain from the straw. The thresher would blow the straw out for storing, and the grain would go into a machine that bagged it.

"Sometimes I would be operating the bagging machine. It would put two bushels of wheat in a bag, and a bushel weighed about 62 pounds, that means 124 pounds, and I weighed 140 pounds, and I'd be handling those all day long, and stack them about as tall as I am."

He worked with his friend, Harry Rheubottom. Work started at seven. But a farm could be five miles away. So they'd get up early, walk five miles to work, hurl 124-pound bags for 10 hours, then walk five miles home, get up the next day and do it again, working hard pretty much non-stop, except a break at lunch.

"The farmer would always provide lunch for the people who were working in the threshing operation," he says. "The whites would usually eat in the kitchen or some place. We ate maybe out on the porch, but not in the same room. That's the way it was. You knew where you were supposed to eat."

When the threshing ended, he took regular day work, which involved pitchforks and dropped the rate from 15 to 10 cents an hour. And then one day a farmer said, "Boy, you know a nigger ain't got sense enough to teach."

If he told Carrie about that, she would have told him what she always told him.

"You pay that no mind. That doesn't define who you are. You determine who you are. You be about your business."

Warren went about his business. He quit that Friday and headed out of town Saturday. He'd made more than $60 that summer. Tuition was $126 a year. He would need money for books, food, fees, maybe some clothes, and getting around. And a place to live.

He packed everything he owned into a handbag. He couldn't afford a train and didn't have access to a car. He approached Henry Forsythe, who owned a store on Main Street, and asked for a lift to Baltimore. Every Saturday, Forsythe went into Baltimore to stock his store, and this Saturday he took Warren along.

Warren says, "He was going to Baltimore to buy groceries and supplies. I was chasing a dream."

Henry Forsythe dropped Warren off in Baltimore, did his shopping, and headed home. About a week later, Main Street Sykesville caught fire. The wind blew hard that day. The kids were in school. The fire jumped from roof to roof all along the first block. The fire burned more than two hours and continued to smolder and spew embers deep into the afternoon. It might have gone further, it might have crossed the street and taken the whole town, but the brick building at the end of the first block, the failed bank that was now a pharmacy, slowed the blaze.

The town smelled of burned wood and ruin for a long time. It was the second major fire in 17 years. The fire started in Henry Forsythe's store and completely destroyed it.

Shortly after Warren was born, a fire destroyed Wade Warfield's mill. Shortly after he left, another fire incinerated Main Street. His life in Sykesville had been punctuated by fire. But that life was over.

Thelma

Warren was 17 when Henry Forsythe let him off downtown at Pratt and Fulton. Warren headed north with his suitcase and a specific destination in Northwest Baltimore in mind. He wasn't the first of Carrie's kids to strike out for college in Baltimore. Thelma beat him to that.

Thelma was the fourth child and oldest girl, nine years older than Warren. She'd paid the dollar a week for Mae and Warren to ride the bus to high school. She was born in 1911 and began her schooling in 1916 in the same one-room school as Warren. When Warren rang her doorbell that day in 1937, she was 26.

Robert Moton opened too late for Thelma. There were no high schools for blacks west of Baltimore. So after grade school, Thelma moved to Fairmount Heights, just outside the city limits of Washington, D.C., and lived with her father's sister, Emma. She completed junior high there and started in at Dunbar High School. She completed one year, but then for reasons that didn't make much sense, Ed called her back to Sykesville.

Warren says, "Sometimes my daddy imagined people were doing stuff they never dreamed of doing, and he decided Thelma was running around Washington instead of going to school."

She wasn't. But Ed forced Thelma to abandon her city life and come home, where the nearest high school for black girls was Frederick Douglass in Baltimore. Thelma had no intention of staying in Sykesville and working as a housemaid for white women. All she needed was an address in the city. Carrie's brother Roy lived in Baltimore, and he gave her one. And Thelma was off again.

She stayed with her parents, but every school day starting in 1926 and ending in 1928, she got up before the sun, took care of her chores, gathered her books, dressed, walked down the hill to the train station, and rode out on the six o'clock train. She couldn't afford the fare, but her brothers Russell and Everett worked on repair gangs for the B&O, and the family got free passes.

She sat by herself in the colored section, slept, did her homework, stared out the windows, got off at Camden Station, and walked north to Frederick Douglass High School at Baker and Calhoun Streets.

At the end of the day, she'd head back downtown with her books and onto the train home. Most days she left in dark and got home in dark more than 12 hours later.

She graduated in 1928 and headed straight into a two-year program at Coppin Normal School in Baltimore that prepared young black people to teach in the black elementary schools.

She lived with a Jewish family in Catonsville, just west of Baltimore, as a live-in maid, and worked for room and board and bus fare. She attended school during the day, cleaned house and studied nights and weekends, took the streetcar from Catonsville to Baltimore and back, and after two years, graduated and began teaching.

Eventually, she attended night school at Morgan and got her bachelor's, and later went on to get her master's from New York University.

She would have preferred staying local for the master's program, but Maryland would not admit blacks into the state universities. To avoid potential lawsuits that might force them to integrate the state colleges, the state was willing to pay for black teachers to go to college elsewhere.

"New York University had a program where out-of-state people could come on weekends," Warren says.

"Maryland paid her transportation to New York. They paid her hotel bill to stay the weekend. They paid her tuition. They paid for all her fees and books until Thelma got her master's degree."

Then one day in September of 1937, she heard someone at her door at 1825 Presstman Street and found Warren with his small bag full of everything he owned. She took one look and said, "I know why you're here."

By then, she'd been teaching in city schools since 1930 and married Sam Jackson. They'd bought a small house. Sam worked at Bethlehem Steel in Sparrow's Point, Baltimore County. Soon the plant would stretch over four miles and become the largest steel mill in the world, but not yet. That would require a war. Right now, there was a Depression, and business was way down.

Rather than lay off workers, they put them on reduced hours. Sam worked a day, maybe two a week. Thelma taught school. They needed two incomes to meet the mortgage. They had no money to spare.

She brought Warren in anyway. She would give him a room and meals, but no money. He'd have to take care of that himself. Which was fine.

He says, "When I left home, I was chasing a dream, but not just my dream. It was my mother's dream, and I was determined to do this for her, and if I couldn't stay at Thelma's, I would find somewhere else. It never crossed my mind I could fail."

He had $115 and somewhere to stay, but was still short a few bucks for tuition, books, and transportation. The

Saturday before registration, he visited the guy at Morgan in charge of scholarships.

"I laid out my sad story, and he told me, 'I don't know if we have any money, but you come register, and when you get where you have to pay, come see me.' When I went to see him, he told me there was a scholarship available. Fifty bucks. Now I had enough for tuition and enough for books."

He was all set. Except it was September 1937, and two years later, on September 1, 1939, as bombs fell and sirens wailed, German troops poured into Poland. Britain and France immediately declared war on Germany. Australia, India, New Zealand, and Canada followed suit.

In the years to come, Mae Dorsey's husband, Harry Whiten, along with Chester Dorsey, Emerson Dorsey, Sam Jackson, and Warren Dorsey would be called by the military. A cloud of dread and fear hung over the world and cast a pall over Warren's future. But ultimately, it wouldn't be the war that stood between him and graduation; it would be something to do with his lungs.

LOVE AND WAR

In 1937, after Thelma let him in with his scholarships and his savings, Warren got rolling at Morgan. You got straight As, you got free tuition. Usually he got free tuition. It's Morgan State University today. Then, it was Morgan College. The president of the school was white. The head of the chemistry department was white, a white lady taught Warren public speaking, but most of the faculty and all of the students were black.

It was an urban school, maybe 600 students, boys and girls both, many of them city residents who commuted to school by streetcar or bus or what they called jitney cab, which was basically a young guy with an entrepreneurial spirit and a car.

Warren says, "He would go around and pick up kids and haul us out there for the same fare you'd pay on a streetcar. Ten cents each way. He'd have a car full, as many as eight of us. That means the ones in the back, somebody was sitting on their laps."

So for a dollar a week, most days Warren rode to college on someone's lap, except when someone sat on his.

He was great at math. Sometimes the head of the math department let him teach class. He taught solid geometry, first-year calculus, analytical geometry, and eventually earned enough credits for a math degree. But he majored in biology instead. He doesn't remember why. Whatever the reason, he eventually took a class in microbiology.

Dr. Monroe, the head of the microbiology department, had a contract with the Baltimore City Health Department to perform clinical testing on samples from the public health clinics, and soon Warren and his classmates were examining blood for bacterial infection, and eventually small things under microscopes became the focus of Warren's life.

He shifted his emphasis to microbiology. He got those As and cruised through freshman and sophomore year. But even with the free money and place to stay, there were carfare and clothes and books and necessities and barely enough to cover it all.

His parents never sent a dollar. Thelma had nothing to spare, and when he wasn't in class or studying, Warren mostly worked. He scrubbed floors and washed windows for a dollar a day. For a few more dollars, he did odd jobs and yard work for a wealthy family that once owned a triple-A version of the Orioles.

Baltimore had a big and growing black population. By 1937, it was more than 145,000, and the center of that black culture and commerce was Pennsylvania Avenue.

They called it "The Avenue," and senior year, Warren landed a job there selling tickets nights and weekends at the Strand Ballroom above the Royal Theater. The Strand was a dance hall. The Royal, downstairs, was a performance theater and part of what they called the chitlin' circuit during the days of Jim Crow, a string of nightclubs, bars, and dancehalls, where black entertainers could come and entertain black people without the danger, overt hostility, and general harassment they'd get anywhere else.

There were also the Apollo Theater and Cotton Club in New York, the Uptown Theater in Philadelphia, the Howard in Washington, the Hippodrome in Richmond, the Regal in Chicago. The chitlin' circuit helped spread the blues and rock & roll, and would someday help launch the brief, brilliant career of Jimi Hendrix, but in Warren's day, the Royal was mostly big band jazz. Count Basie came to play. Duke Ellington came to play. Cab Calloway, Nat King Cole, Ella Fitzgerald, Billie Holliday.

Warren sold tickets. Sometimes he'd sneak in and watch. He particularly enjoyed Louis Armstrong.

"Louis Armstrong was a crowd pleaser. When his group set up for a concert, he never left the grandstand or the stage as long as the performance was in session. The others would come and do a couple sets and they would disappear."

The Royal, with room for a thousand patrons, showed movies, once hosted a boxing exhibition by black champion Jack Johnson, and put on a full vaudeville show with a band, comedians, and a chorus line. The Strand was just dancing. Armstrong played both.

It was only a mile and a half from Thelma's place, an easy walk by Warren's standards, who walked just about everywhere, but Warren mostly just worked there. He didn't hang out on the Avenue. He didn't have the time, didn't have the money, and didn't really have the inclination. To this day, he's never had a drink, never smoked a cigarette, and is not likely to start now.

Besides, Thelma would have frowned on it. Carrie would have scorned it. So Warren worked the Strand, went to watch Morgan play their home basketball games in an arena on the Avenue, had a couple hot dogs and a coke for 50 cents after the games, and headed home to Thelma's, where he slept and studied and ate most of his meals.

Summers were much less exciting. Warren needed money, which meant full-time work, and full-time work usually meant drudgery, but anything beat going back to the farm.

"I promised my good Lord when I left I would never work on the farm again, unless I got awful hungry," he says. "I hadn't gotten that hungry yet. The first summer after I started Morgan, I tried working in the city, and I went to an employment agency on Pennsylvania Avenue. You register and sit and wait for a job, and I sat two weeks and never got a single job."

One summer he worked at a factory making boxes, mostly for cigarettes, in Ilchester, outside Ellicott City in Howard County. Another, he worked cleaning up at a kitchen on the University of Maryland campus for a while, before his brother Rom got him a job washing pots and pans and preparing vegetables at Henryton.

And somehow or another he mostly stayed off the farm and managed to collect enough for tuition and getting by.

In school he continued to excel at math, but mostly he studied microbes and bacteria. He stared through microscopes and dreamt of emulating George Washington Carver, a great black biochemist born during the Civil War.

Warren thought he might do big things himself, like Carver, only different. Carver's idea was to grow what most suited the soil and make that profitable. Warren's was to take the small things all around us, microbes mainly, bacteria, stuff we can't see, and use them to improve the soil. But one day, some of that mysterious stuff we can't see got in his lungs.

It hit early junior year, some sort of respiratory infection. Every breath hurt. Fluid built up around his lungs. Soon he couldn't work or study or go to school. He tested negative for TB. He didn't have pneumonia. Whatever he had, he could barely get out of bed.

He saw a doctor, a black man named Hugh Price Hughes, who charged $2.25 a visit. When Warren's money ran out, the doctor treated him awhile, but the illness persisted beyond the doctor's charity, and eventually Dr. Hughes suggested a clinic at Johns Hopkins Hospital in East Baltimore far from Thelma's house.

In her great book, *The Immortal Life of Henrietta Lacks*, Rebecca Skloot tells the story of Henrietta Lacks, a poor black woman from Baltimore who died a miserable death in Johns Hopkins Hospital in 1951. Mostly abandoned, mostly alone, her guts burnt black with the radiation they fired at her tumors, Henrietta Lacks died of cervical cancer.

Except one part of her didn't, the monster thing, the cells that killed her and didn't die with her. They lived on. They're alive today. They're called HeLa cells, and scientists buy them and study them and hope to use them to cure disease.

Before her diagnosis, when Henrietta couldn't stand her symptoms anymore, her husband, David, took her to a clinic at Hopkins.

Skloot writes, "Hopkins was one of the top hospitals in the country. It was built in 1889 as a charity hospital for the sick and poor, and it covered more than a dozen acres where a cemetery and insane asylum once sat in East Baltimore. The public wards at Hopkins were filled with patients, most of them black and unable to pay their medical bills.

"David drove Henrietta nearly twenty miles to get there, not because they preferred it, but because it was the only major hospital for miles that treated black patients. This was the era of Jim Crow—when black people showed up at white-only hospitals, the staff was likely to send them away, even if it meant they might die in the parking lot. Even Hopkins, which did treat black patients, segregated them in colored wards, and had colored-only fountains."

When Warren got sick, this is where he dragged himself, that exact same clinic for the sick and poor where David took Henrietta. Warren was one of those patients, always black and unable to pay, who filled the public wards at Hopkins. It's doubtful much changed at the clinic for better or worse between 1942, when Warren was a regular, and 1951, when Henrietta showed up to die and change the history of medicine and humanity.

Warren lived at Thelma's near North Avenue in West Baltimore, and the hospital was a long ways off in East Baltimore. If he had money, he took the streetcar. If he didn't, he walked, maybe an hour, maybe more, so sick he could barely get out of bed.

The facility itself was much nicer than the experience of being there. Warren arrived at nine o'clock each morning and sat, usually for hours, among the sick with no other choice. Men, women, children. Old and young. Sneezing, wheezing, hacking; stooped and miserable; no doubt suffering everything from common colds to cancer and tuberculosis. And he was hungry and tired and weak and worried, and every visit he went through the same routine.

He says, "You wait till a social worker interviews you, trying to establish that you're destitute and qualified for a free clinic. And sometimes it would be afternoon before you got to see a doctor.

"A couple times I came down with pleurisy. It's a fluid build-up around the lungs and it's very debilitating. I was hospitalized on two different occasions to have fluid drained from my lung area with a hypodermic. You stayed over, and the next day they let you go home. That didn't cost me anything, but I had a rough time for a little while."

It didn't cost money, but there was a price. You weren't exactly a guinea pig or a lab rat, they didn't experiment on you, but you were on display.

He'd be on a bed in a gown in a room and doctors would come in with students, maybe eight or 10 around the bed. So while Warren lay there exhausted and ill, he was poked and prodded, discussed and analyzed by students and professors.

He was, Warren says, "It." The thing. No one made eye contact with him. No one said hello or gave him a smile. They took turns taking his pulse, putting stethoscopes to his heart, listening to his chest, discussing his condition and their conclusions.

It didn't bother him much. He was sick. He wanted help. He was grateful for the attention, but he wasn't getting better, and eventually he couldn't take it anymore. On the fifth of November, he told the school he was dropping out and heading home to Sykesville.

He says, "It was actually December before I could go back up to Sykesville, and as soon as I thought I could work, I went back to the box factory to earn money to get back to school.

"But when I went back to school the next year, the same thing happened all over, and I came back home to get well again, and I guess my mother said something to Margaret Harris, who had some connection with the agency that placed youngsters in the Civilian Conservation Corps. I registered and was sent to a camp in Beltsville."

The Civilian Conservation Corps, or CCC, was one of President Roosevelt's New Deal programs for alleviating the unemployment crisis during the Depression. The idea was to get young men off the streets, provide some economic relief for the nation's rural poor, and do valuable work. Eventually some three million men would plant trees, restore historic battlefields, build wildlife shelters, dig ditches and canals, and stock rivers and streams with fish.

The CCC was under control of the army and provided some good practice for what was coming. For one thing, you called your superiors "sir."

"The Agricultural Department ran a farm there, and they had various kinds of experiments, animals, plants, and all," Warren says. "They owned quite a bit of acreage, and the fellows in the CCC camp took care of the acreage."

Warren was no longer fond of taking care of acreage. But in the CCC, he wouldn't be taking care of any acreage. He wouldn't be clearing forests, building bridges, planting any of those million trees, or getting much of the vigorous outdoor exercise the CCC intended to promote, either.

Like his dad, cooking for the wrecking crews in the rail yards of Baltimore, Warren got himself a cushy job. He ran the snack bar for the tree cutters and trail builders. He sold snacks at night from the time the workers got off till nine. The hours were short, the work was light. He managed the stock, talked to salespeople, served up sodas, and rarely broke a sweat.

"For two summers I did that and both summers I ended up running the canteen."

Chiseling Ds

There's one other thing he did. It was the summer of '42, nearly 100 years after Aunt Kitty was born, and Ed got hold of some sort of hand-operated machine that made concrete blocks, and decided he would get in early on a boom in the building industry. The boom ended after about a dozen blocks, but Ed had those blocks and then he got another idea.

He had Warren take four blocks and chisel a D in the top of each. Then Ed, Warren, and his brother Chester hopped in Chester's car and drove off to the Bushy Park Cemetery. It was a short ride.

When they got there, Ed measured off the distance, then had Warren and Chester dig four holes and drop a concrete block in each with a D facing up, thereby claiming a rectangular plot of grass with a specific, if not cheerful, purpose.

Whether Ed actually had the right to claim that ground, Warren isn't sure, but he did, and that's where Ed established the Ed Dorsey family burial ground.

Chickens

He came close, but Warren never did completely escape working at the home place during his college years. It's just that the work he did there, on and off, during those years had very little to do with farming the land and a lot to do with chickens.

Rom was an idea man, so maybe it was his idea, or maybe it was Chester's, or maybe Thelma's husband, Sam, came up with it, but one of them decided they should become chicken tycoons, or egg barons, or whatever it is you become when you raise chickens and sell chickens and eggs by the thousands.

They set up operations behind the house sometime in the late thirties. They didn't give themselves a name, but Rom, Chester, and Sam went into the chicken and egg business, with the chickens coming first.

They bought a few old buildings someone was tearing down, hauled the lumber up to the farm, and built a long structure of sorts that would hold more than a thousand layers, which is chicken-farmer lingo for hens that lay eggs.

They also built a few other wooden houses and filled them with starter chicks they bought at hatcheries. They cared for the starters, grew them, sold off the cockerels, and turned the pullets into more layers once they got old enough.

In chicken-farmer lingo, which Warren speaks fluently, cockerels are young roosters, and pullets are hens too young to lay eggs. So the pullets became hens, which laid eggs, and the cockerels became roosters, which became dinner for tuberculosis patients.

He says, "We had individual brooder houses where we started chickens. When you got the baby chicks from the hatchery, you started them out in the brooder houses that would hold maybe about 500. Each brooder house had a brooder stove, and you had to keep the fire going to provide warmth for the chickens."

Rom made a deal with Henryton. The unnamed Dorsey chicken and egg factory provided Henryton with fresh eggs and fresh cockerels. Once the cockerels were big enough, they killed them, and Warren, who often helped with the operation, killed hundreds of young roosters in his day. There was nothing fancy about it. You hung them by the feet a few at a time, then slit their throats with a knife.

He says, "We supplied Henryton something around 200 or 300 cockerels at a time. A bunch of us would kill the chickens, pick them, and take them to Henryton. Every week we supplied two or three crates of eggs."

They had their challenges initially getting the business off the ground.

Warren says, "It was common practice for farmers to deal with people who supply cattle and poultry feed, and the suppliers would deliver the feed during the month as you needed it, and you paid at the end of the month. But the feed store in Sykesville, Maryland Milling and Supply, wouldn't make such an arrangement with the Dorseys. Sykesville was not a very friendly town based upon race when I was there."

In other words, Maryland Milling and Supply, Wade Warfield's old company, wouldn't extend credit to the Dorseys because they were black. But a friend of Chester's in town, a white man named Gene Berry, hooked them up on good terms with a feed company in Ellicott City that let them pay at the end of the month. They had their feed. They had their chickens. They had their customer.

"It was fairly profitable," Warren says. "But Sam was inducted in 1942 or early '43. Ches was inducted in 1943, and Rom had the accident with his hand."

The operation began around 1935 and folded sometime in 1942, another victim of Adolph Hitler's war to purify humanity.

The United States Is at War

While the brothers sold chickens and eggs and Warren struggled with his health and his finances, Europe struggled with the Luftwaffe and blitzkrieg and the Fuehrer's unstoppable armies. In June 1940, the French surrendered. The most powerful army between Hitler and domination of Western Europe was cut off, defeated, and dead.

Poland, Austria, Czechoslovakia, Denmark, Norway, Belgium, The Netherlands, Luxembourg, and France were soon under Nazi rule. Standing alone across the English Channel lay Britain. It had airplanes. It had ships. It had Churchill and the Channel and a desperate hope that if it could hold out long enough, America would enter the war on its side. But Americans did not want to enter the war.

With the French beaten, Hitler launched a massive air campaign in July 1940. They bombed London, Liverpool, Birmingham, Manchester, Nottingham, Bristol, and several other British cities. Air raid sirens shrieked at night. Citizens waited in tube stations in underground London for the sirens and the rumbling and explosions to stop, only to emerge and fight fire and injury and death. They shipped thousands of children out to the countryside.

Buildings fell, people died, sirens screamed, people screamed, planes exploded and splashed smoking into the Channel. Churchill spoke to his people.

"Even though large tracts of Europe and many old and famous States have fallen or may fall into the grip of the Gestapo and all the odious apparatus of Nazi rule, we shall not flag or fail. We shall go on to the end. We shall fight in France, we shall fight on the seas and oceans, we shall fight with growing confidence and growing strength in the air, we shall defend our island, whatever the cost may be.

"We shall fight on the beaches, we shall fight on the landing grounds, we shall fight in the fields and in the streets, we shall fight in the hills; we shall never surrender."

The battle continued to the end of October. More than 23,000 British civilians died, another 30,000 were injured. Both the Luftwaffe and the Royal Air Force lost thousands of planes. England did not surrender. And the United States did not enter the war.

The British stalled Hitler. He couldn't cross the Channel. He couldn't defeat the British Air Force. He had predicted a thousand-year reign for his Third Reich. He seemed poised to rule much of Europe for decades, but thwarted by England and Churchill, he changed direction, and in the hour before dawn in June 1941, he sent four million troops over the border into the Soviet Union.

Warren worked his jobs. He concentrated on school and tried to stay well. He hoped the U.S. would stay out, but then came that famous Sunday in December 1941. He'd come up from Baltimore with Thelma and Sam to visit his parents. He was out walking the fields with Emerson.

In the house was a radio, an Atwater Kent they'd bought from Asa Hepner not long after they finally got electricity up Oklahoma Hill. It was a big old console with hot glowing tubes inside. It sat in the dining room, which caught just enough heat from the kitchen stove to make it tolerable in winter.

All through the thirties, the family would gather around that radio. They would listen to Amos 'n' Andy and Buck Rogers. And whenever the rabble-rousing Father Coughlin, a Catholic priest with his own radio show and millions of listeners came on, Ed would appear from his room and listen closely as the controversial Coughlin attacked FDR, "the heinous rottenness of modern capitalism," and the vile Godlessness of communism, too.

And on the radio that day on December 7, 1941, word came in, and someone ran out to the field and broke the news to Warren and Emerson. The Japanese had just launched 414 planes at a place in Hawaii called Pearl Harbor. More than 2400 Americans were dead, thousands were wounded, and mighty ships burned and sank and spewed smoke into the sky.

Our Pacific fleet was crippled. The Japanese had accomplished what Churchill and Roosevelt couldn't. They had made up our mind. The United States declared war on Japan. And then Germany and Italy.

Under the headline, "United We Stand," the *Sykesville Herald* wrote:

"The conflict, which was inevitable, has come to our shores. For the seventh time in our history as a nation, the United States is at war."

The Reverend Karl B. Justus wrote on the *Herald's* front page.

"We now find ourselves embroiled in the Second World War. Though this may not be to our liking, it is the real fact of that which seemed inevitable. We must forget our likes and dislikes; we must join the call of our President, regardless of party or politics, in a national unity invincible; and we must prepare ourselves to meet untold sacrifice."

Justus was the pastor of St. Paul's Church. He would soon go to war as a chaplain and come back months later a deeply changed and troubled man. He gave his last sermon on Sunday, December 6, 1942, to a packed church with people of every congregation and faith and the front pews filled with firemen, minutemen, and members of the civilian defense core wearing uniforms and armbands.

Gasoline, butter, sugar, coffee, tires, solid fuels, shoes, kerosene, meats, and other necessities would soon be rationed. Air raid sirens were tested. Blackouts were practiced. Windows were darkened at night. Trains rattled past the ghostly dark town while residents gathered around tube radios and listened for encouraging news, which at first did not come at all.

Roosevelt gave fireside chats over radio. He provided calm leadership. His legs were crippled with polio. He would go into war vibrant and young. He would have come out withered and ill, but instead, he did not come out at all. But that was yet to come, and week after week, Sykesville opened its paper and read about its sons in France or in ships going island to island in the Pacific.

Beginning in November 1943, the *Herald* included a front-page section called "With Those In The Service." It was filled with tales of local soldiers stationed all over the world.

In January 1944, the *Herald* reported that Lt. Gerald B. Lyons was the first local boy to die in combat. In his last letter home, Lyons wrote from the Fiji Islands:

"The Japs have been bombing us rather heavily. Keep your chin up and don't worry about me. I know how to take care of myself."

On February 3, 1944, the *Herald* wrote lamenting "the grim reality that the war is a long way from being won" and complained of the draft's constant drain on the men of the community.

"This week several more men from Sykesville's thinning ranks passed their final physicals and were accepted to military service to begin sometime within 20 to 90 days."

Not long after, another boy from Sykesville died. His name was Gurney Davis. He left behind a wife and a two-year-old daughter.

On February 15, 1945, the *Herald* wrote of Sykesville's first colored officer, a new second lieutenant named Sergeant J. Sidney Sheppard who had just graduated the Officers' Training School at Camp Lee, Virginia.

"Lt. Sheppard is the first of the colored soldiers from this area to have this honor. He is the son of the late Levi Sheppard and Mrs. Queenetta Sheppard, of the White Rock Community...Lt. Sheppard was among more than 200 new officers graduated from the Quartermaster School at Camp Lee."

In that same issue, they told the story of First Lieutenant John R. Arrington, a bomber pilot from Marriottsville. His family had just received a telegram from the War Department. Arrington's B-24 bomber had crashed in Norfolk, England. He died in the explosion.

The Germans finally surrendered that May. The Japanese surrendered in September, but on August 7, the *Herald* reported that Captain Wayne L. Flohr, a graduate of Sykesville High, the pilot of a B-24 Liberator bomber, and a member of St. Paul's United Methodist Church, had died in a flying accident over India.

The war was all but over when his wife, Audrey, got word at her home in Catonsville.

He was the last from Sykesville to die in the war.

Around the world, some 80 million died, 50 million of them civilians. More than seven million Germans, three million Japanese, between 20 and 30 million Russians, nearly half a million Americans, more than five million Poles, and six million Jews who died in the most horrible of ways.

Very few of the half-million American dead were from Sykesville, but Sykesville was a town of very few.

The Gentle Giant

When the Japanese hit Pearl Harbor, Mae, who'd once hid her bloomers in a tree, was now Mae Whiten, and her husband, Harry, was stationed stateside with the army and anxious to get home. He had a month left on a one-year stint, but after the planes came and the ships burned, instead of home, Harry was off to the South Pacific.

Thelma's husband, Sam, was no longer scraping for work at Bethlehem Steel. Business boomed, but soon Sam, too, was on his way to the South Pacific.

Then Chester Dorsey, the oldest of the three youngest Dorsey boys, followed Harry and Sam, but rather than the South Pacific, he landed in India as a cook.

Chester was married to a local girl from Oklahoma Hill. Her name was Minnie. Minnie's dad was Hagen Bond, the truck driver from Maryland Milling and Supply, who timed his rides to give Mae, Warren, and the others a lift to school.

Minnie was born in 1923, and when she was 13, Warren took her to the prom. She had so much fun at the prom with Warren that she married his brother Chester. And the army sent Chester to the war.

They shouldn't have. There were two reasons. One, he should have been dead. Two, he was barely recovered from the accident that should have killed him when they shipped him off.

Chester was three years older than Warren. He, Emerson, and Warren were the last of the boys and the best of friends. For many years they shared the same bed, the same straw mattress, the same flies and bed bugs, the same frigid winter mornings and stifling summer nights. And while Warren had mostly good luck, Chester's was the opposite, and in October 1940, when Chester was 24, a truck jackknifed, turned over, and crushed his car.

The *Herald* covered it on the front page of the October 3, 1940, issue. Amazingly, there were two separate fatal accidents reported on the front page that day. Each involved a truck. Each involved a car filled with young blacks from the Sykesville area, and in each car there was at least one young Dorsey.

They printed the first accident above the second because in that one two men died, including 21-year-old Douglas Dorsey, whom Dr. H. A. Barnes pronounced dead, at the scene, of a fractured skull. His parents were John and Genevieve Dorsey, unrelated to Warren's family, but not unfamiliar. John Dorsey was the first man to encourage Warren's singing, and after Warren's family moved out of the house behind Main Street where Carrie had paid rent by doing the owner's laundry, John and Genevieve Dorsey moved in. (The house was later destroyed in a fire, but both Dorsey families had moved on by then.)

Of Chester's accident, the *Herald* wrote: "Four colored persons were injured Tuesday night when the automobile in which they were riding was sideswiped by a large trailer truck on the Liberty Road near North Branch.

"The injured, all occupants of a Ford coach which was demolished by the crash, were: Chester Dorsey, driver, three broken ribs and punctured lung; Sally Miller, in charge of nurses at Henryton sanatorium, broken hip; Joe Dorsey, cook at Springfield Hospital, cut and bruises about head; his wife, undetermined injuries."

The unnamed wife of Joe Dorsey, also unrelated to Warren's family, eventually died of her unnamed injuries. Sally Miller had two broken ankles, but of the survivors, Chester had the worst of it.

"They took Ches to University Hospital in Baltimore," Warren says. "And when we saw him that night, they weren't expecting him to survive. He had a crushed chest, punctured lung, broken ribs."

Chester was the biggest of them all. At 15, he stood at six foot-four and 200 pounds, an entire foot taller than his older brother, Russell. He towered over Warren and Emerson. He was big, strong, powerful, smart, and terrifically athletic. He was an excellent pitcher, who might have been good enough to play in the negro leagues if he'd had more discipline and more desire and less of an inclination to pitch the way he wanted and not how someone might tell him to.

Warren says, "The five youngest kids, from Mae on down, we all looked up to Ches. Ches was our protector. He was our idol. He helped provide for us. He was everything to us. He was a giant, a gentle giant."

And now he was in a hospital bed and most likely not going to make it.

"For a long while, it was touch and go. He was in the hospital until February, and the doctors predicted the army wouldn't take him."

It took more than four months, but Chester healed. He married Minnie in 1941. They built a small green house beside the family farmhouse. It's still there today, and so is Minnie, and despite the doctor's prediction, the army did take Chester. By then he was a father of two. His son, Chester, Jr., was born in 1942, followed quickly by Patsy, who came along while Chester was in India.

Not long after arriving in India, Chester got sick. They didn't know what it was. He wasn't the first to contract the illness, and it killed most of them. They suspected some sort of foreign strain of diphtheria, but weren't sure, and surely didn't know what to do about it. As he became more ill, he wrote Thelma. He told her he might be dying. He asked her, please don't tell Minnie or Carrie.

Finally he collapsed. He lost his vision. He lost all ability to communicate. He couldn't move at all. He lay in India alone, paralyzed, and blind. At one point, someone ordered him shipped out, but before the plane took off, a doctor stopped it, and warned the pilot.

"You have a man on board. If you take off, he's going to die."

So Chester stayed in India, trapped, his mind alert, but slowly fading. Eventually, Minnie received a notice from the military authorities. She read it and ran next door to Carrie.

Number Two Joins the Army

Soon the government started drafting kids out of college. Warren's health was still poor. It took him three years to complete junior year. Now he had a choice, enlist or be drafted. If you enlisted, you could complete your schooling. So in August 1942, Warren enlisted in the Reserve Corp of the United States Army.

Then the deal changed. We were fighting in Africa, fighting in the Pacific, preparing to invade Italy, and now, in college or not, you were subject to the draft. Only certain majors were exempt. Biology was one. As the classrooms emptied, as the campus grew lonely and deserted, Warren stayed on, grimly pursuing his goal.

And in June 1943, six years after riding out of Sykesville with Henry Forsythe, 22-year-old Warren Dorsey graduated from Morgan College with a Bachelor of Science in Biology. He was not number one in his class. That honor went to Ezell W. Johnson, a young black woman from Chattanooga, Tennessee. Warren finished second.

He says, "Here I was, this little old country boy from this little high school with only two teachers, competing with kids out of New Jersey and Pennsylvania and Baltimore and succeeding through pure determination. I'd accomplished the dream.

"But it wasn't my dream particularly, it was mostly my mother's dream. She wanted her kids to get educated and get away from Sykesville. That was my mission, that was my main motivation, to achieve my mother's dream, and that's what I did."

Carrie was thrilled. She came to Baltimore and watched with Thelma as, for the first time, one of her sons graduated from college, number two in his class.

Ed stayed home, inscrutable, mysterious, and silent.

Warren says, "Ed never once said a thing to me about my going to school."

A Mile Never Walked

Warren loved his country. It was something Miss Bell instilled in him many years ago. But he never planned on being a soldier. He had bigger plans, and better.

He'd been granted a fellowship by the Rosenwald Foundation, a philanthropic organization established in 1917 for the well-being of mankind by Julius Rosenwald, the President of Sears, Roebuck and Company. The foundation gave scholarships to black students, including Warren, who was accepted into a graduate program and intended to work toward his doctorate.

He says, "I'd planned to pursue humanitarian work improving marginal farmland by using microbiological enrichment. The goal was to help poor farmers who tilled marginally productive land. The vast majority of African-American farmers worked such land. I wanted to help people like my own family."

But first came the army. They gave him two weeks after graduation and then called him in. Helping poor black farmers would have to wait. Forever, as it turned out.

He reported to the reception center at Fort Meade, not all that far from Baltimore, in June 1943. Meade was supposed to be a quick stop, but Warren was a young black man with a college degree, a history of recent illness, and bad eyes, all of which seemed to gum up the system.

They held him two and a half months before finally deciding he was suited for limited service only. They sent him from Fort Meade to Camp Lee, just outside Petersburg, Virginia, in the process, transferring him from a place named after General George G. Meade, who led the Union forces to victory at Gettysburg, to a place named after General Robert E. Lee, who led the Confederate troops to disaster.

It was at Petersburg that General Ulysses S. Grant faced down Lee's army, laid siege to the city, and after nine months of brutal trench warfare, with 42,000 Union casualties and 28,000 Confederate, finally took the town on April 2, 1865.

Richmond fell soon after. Lee surrendered. Lincoln had freed millions of slaves with his Emancipation Proclamation. Soon the rest were freed, and the Thirteenth, Fourteenth, and Fifteenth Amendments theoretically solidified their rights.

By the late 1860s, blacks were equal citizens of the United States. Warren arrived at Camp Lee 80 years later and took up residence with the colored troops in the colored barracks in the totally segregated American army.

Camp Lee was the Quartermaster Replacement Training Center. They were basically all support troops and that meant things like driving trucks, shuffling papers, and registering graves.

Warren had a bachelor of science. Today most college graduates become officers, but at Camp Lee in 1943, that was not necessarily the case. The commanding officer was white. The head of each platoon was white. Most officers were white.

And Warren was not the only African-American college graduate at Camp Lee. Among the black troops, all the non-commissioned officers were black and almost all were college graduates.

Warren remembers, "I met a black Ph.D. there from Harvard, and his job was to count the troops coming in and out of the cafeteria. That was the best they could do for him."

Warren did not have a Ph.D. from Harvard, and arriving a bit later in the war, he was eligible for Officer Candidate School. He did well on the test and was initially accepted into the program, but with his bad eyes and suspect health they eventually turned him down.

So with his bachelor's in biology, his advanced skills in mathematics, and his fellowship to pursue a doctorate in microbiology, Warren went through clerical training, graduated, and then they made him a drill sergeant.

And he was good at it, too. He says, "I could do it again, right now, if I had to."

Life in the army wasn't all bad. Thirty dollars a month, a few sets of matching clothes, real underwear made by professionals, good shoes, training, a place to stay, something to eat, a Ph.D. from Harvard to count you on your way in and out of the mess hall. And dental care.

In her book tracking expenses, Carrie mentions several 75-cent expenditures for pulling a tooth, but none of those 75-cent tooth expenditures were expended on Warren. Warren had never seen a dentist in his life from more than a distance, which may have been a good thing. The dentist in Sykesville, a man named Waesche, would not treat black patients in his office, but they could go to him after-hours.

In her book on Sykesville, Linda Greenberg writes: "In the 1920s younger patients such as Russell Shipley, recalled dreading the slow-moving, treadle-driven drill that bore into a tooth and created horrible pain. This was before the days of localized anesthetics, such as Novocain, and high-speed, electric powered drills."

So maybe Warren was lucky. But by the time he entered the army, he had a mouth full of rotten teeth and Uncle Sam, who wanted drill sergeants with healthy smiles, fixed them.

Besides bad eyes and the wrong color skin, Warren had another asset that kept him from combat. He could sing. And not long after arriving, he ran into a man named Bennett. They'd sung together in the chorus at Morgan. Bennett told Warren that Colonel Watson, Camp Lee's white commanding officer, had a black glee club, and soon enough Warren became a member of the all-black 9th Regiment glee club.

The commander loved his glee club. If you were in the glee club you weren't going anywhere. In Warren's case, your duties were drilling troops and singing. Often you got called off training duty for singing duty. Sometimes you even sang with someone famous, or nearly so, like Johnny Hartman.

Hartman was from Chicago, a couple years younger than Warren, and like Warren, he'd started out in church choirs, and eventually, like Warren, earned a scholarship. Only Hartman's was to study music at Chicago Musical College.

After the war, Hartman would perform with Earl Hines, Dizzy Gillespie, and Erroll Garner, and in 1963, become the only singer ever to record an album with John Coltrane. He was nominated for a Grammy in 1981 and died in 1983 at 60, but once, when barely 20, he sang in an army glee club with Warren Dorsey.

And didn't like it much. Warren laughs about it. "Johnny thought he was better than we were. And he sort of resented singing with us. But he did it, because if he didn't, he could be shipped out and end up in a combat zone."

A black professor named J. Harold Montague directed the choir and chaired the music department at nearby Virginia State College for Negroes, until Colonel Watson recruited him to enter the army and direct the Camp Lee glee club. Virginia State was just outside Lee, and at the college, one of Montague's most talented singers was a friendly, attractive young soloist named Carolyn Baugh.

Carolyn happened to be on base one night and stepped in and watched Montague's soldiers sing. Maybe she noticed Warren, maybe she didn't. It was 70 years ago and neither remembers their first meeting exactly, but somehow or another they must have had one.

The army operated USO clubs for the servicemen. You could listen to Glenn Miller, you could dance if you could, you could write letters home. Awhile after that rehearsal, where Warren and Carolyn may have met but don't remember, they had another meeting that neither remembers very well, either.

They agree on this much. Warren was sitting in the black USO club in Petersburg when Carolyn approached, or as Warren once put it, "zeroed in on me." Maybe she felt sorry for him, a young soldier by himself, perhaps looking a bit lonely and forlorn, or maybe she still remembered their recent meeting. But for some reason, she zeroed in and asked him to dance. Warren was shy, and if he'd ever danced before, it was only once, and that was in 1937 with the future Minnie Dorsey.

Minnie, who's thin and small and healthy with white hair, had me over one Sunday afternoon in the small green house she built with Chester in 1941, and at Minnie's kitchen table, she and Warren told the story, both of them laughing quite a bit.

Minnie says, "I remember he asked me I'm going to be his date at the prom. I was 13, and my mother and father took me, and his brother, Rom, took him. And he was on one side the room and I was on the other. But we were at the prom."

Warren says, "We sure were."

And Minnie says, "We danced once, didn't we?"

Warren shakes his head, like it's possible, but he's skeptical. "Minnie was a good dancer, but I couldn't dance."

Minnie says, "And his classmates on the other side of the room kept saying, 'he can't dance, he can't dance.'"

The dance was at Robert Moton on the second floor. There were only four classrooms in the whole school and each floor had a collapsible wall to separate the classrooms and create two per floor, which was more than enough, since there were only two teachers.

The night of the prom, they opened the divider on the second floor and brought in a four-piece band. And although Minnie and Warren both agree they were on opposite sides of the room and that Minnie asked Warren to dance, neither remembers whether the dance actually took place before Minnie's parents came for her and Warren's brother came for him.

So first dance or second, Warren danced with Carolyn that night at the USO, and did well enough, because after the dance, she continued to speak to him, even though she was young and smart and talented and educated and a member of a higher social class, and Warren was just some drill sergeant with a big booming voice a few years off the farm from a town no one ever heard of with a recently repaired set of teeth, bad eyes, and not a penny to his name the army didn't give him.

But Warren was also a very smart, educated, funny, and strong, lean, handsome fellow. Maybe he couldn't dance, but he sure could sing, and whether either of them knew it that night, the two of them would be singing together for many years to come.

Carolyn taught in Petersburg. She lived with her parents in a nice house in an all-black neighborhood in a home her father bought from Carolyn's grandmother, in a totally segregated city with a large black population. They had all the modern amenities that Warren's old home lacked: heat, running water, flush toilets.

It was an educated family. Her brothers Billie and Howard both graduated from Virginia State. Another brother, Herb, began at Virginia State but finished at Duquesne. Her sister, Olivette, also finished Virginia State.

Carolyn doesn't know much about the older history of her family. She knows her grandparents were all born after the Civil War, and her dad was born in 1890, her mom in 1893. Her dad was a bricklayer who employed a few men and built buildings. Her mom taught school. All the kids graduated from college, and one of them went down in history. We'll return to him shortly.

Another thing she knows now but didn't know till just a few years before meeting Warren was that she could sing.

She says, "I didn't know I could sing until I was in high school. When they asked for tryouts for the choir I tried out and I got in."

Carolyn's shy now. She doesn't have a lot to say, and is probably being modest when she claims she wasn't really that great a singer.

Warren gets agitated about it. "She was great. She had a terrific soprano voice. She went on to college and became one of the soloists in the choir."

And like Warren, Carolyn had her brush with the soon-to-be famous, only in her case there were two, one a jazz pianist, the other a singer. The pianist was Billy Taylor, another student at Virginia State. He would go on to become one of the most famous jazz personalities in American history, but then he was just a guy in his early twenties.

When he died in 2010 at 89, the New York Times wrote a story about him.

They wrote: "He had his first piano lesson at seven and later studied music at what is now Virginia State University. Shortly after moving to New York in 1943—within two days of his arrival, he later recalled—he began working with the tenor saxophonist Ben Webster at the Three Deuces on 52nd Street, and he remained a fixture on that celebrated nightclub row for many years."

But shortly before leaving for New York and fame and gigs with the famous Ben Webster, while studying at Virginia State, Billy Taylor put together a foursome with three college girls. He played piano. They all sang. They didn't go far, mostly just local dances and that sort of thing, but one of the four was Carolyn Baugh.

And then there's Camilla Williams. Williams, though a couple years older, was also a soloist in the choir at Virginia State with Carolyn. She died in 2012, but not before becoming in 1946, as the New York Times wrote in an obituary, "the first black woman to secure a contract with a major United States opera company."

She would later record George Gershwin's *Porgy and Bess* for Columbia Records and sing solo with several European orchestras, perform with the Vienna State Opera, tour the United States and many other countries, and sing the "Star Spangled Banner" to 200,000 people a few minutes before Martin Luther King, Jr., gave the most famous speech of his life.

So Carolyn sang with Camilla Williams. She sang with Billy Taylor. She sang with two huge stars, but in the end, she did most of her singing with an unknown farm boy from Sykesville.

Wee Goes "Bang"

The family called Warren's younger brother "Wee." No one knows why. Emerson, who died in 2000, was famous for his corny jokes and endless good humor, but joking or not, he was as hard working and ambitious as his older brother. Maybe as smart, too, and their paths off the farm to college and into the military were different and equally challenging.

Emerson was born in 1922. Not long after Warren moved in with Thelma in Baltimore, Emerson found his own hard way forward and graduated college without paying a cent.

In fact, though Warren was first to enter, Emerson and Warren both received their degrees in 1943. Both set off from Sykesville with a suitcase and no sure idea how they were going to pay for their education. Both worked for the Civilian Conservation Corp. Both completed college and entered the army. And eventually, both ended up living and working in the same place in the same town.

But unlike his brother, Emerson didn't have a $50 scholarship. Emerson Jr., who's in his early sixties, remembers how he managed it.

"When he was working in the Civilian Conservation Corps, one of his counselors taught at Princess Anne College and asked Daddy what he was going to do, because Daddy was a hard worker. And Daddy told him he wanted to go to college, but didn't have any money.

"The counselor, or maybe he was some kind of administrator, told Daddy if he really wanted to go, to be at Princess Anne when school started, find him, and he'd make sure Daddy was taken care of."

Princess Anne is now the University of Maryland Eastern Shore. It was one of the three choices available. Warren chose Morgan. Thelma chose Coppin. Emerson traveled around the Chesapeake with no guarantees and no money to Maryland's Eastern Shore, where just a few years earlier, on separate occasions over a couple years, the locals had brutally beaten, lynched, and incinerated two black men, causing outrage across the state.

"Daddy headed off to Princess Anne with his one cardboard suitcase, and sure enough, the man took care of him. Daddy did odd jobs on campus, one being to fire up the furnaces in all of the buildings every morning in the winter. Daddy said after he graduated in 1943, he tallied up all of the work he did, and he figured he didn't owe the school any money. The school owed him."

So Warren got a head start, but Emerson didn't suffer from pleurisy. They both graduated in 1943, and Emerson headed into the military, too.

He was another college-educated black man, and the army didn't really know what to do with him. They assigned him to Fort Bragg, North Carolina, at a school for illiterates, where he tried to teach them to read. They sent him to several different bases. At times he'd be the only black soldier. At a base in Iowa they housed him in the officer's quarters, because they couldn't put a black fellow in the barracks with regular troops. They eventually assigned him to a personnel unit in Florida.

Emerson, Jr., says, "Daddy was a classification specialist. He would fill up groups that would get shipped overseas. Sometimes, they would try to bribe him so they wouldn't be shipped out."

And somewhere along the line, something like this happened. Or at least this is the story Emerson, Sr., told. Warren is skeptical.

Warren says, "On this one base, Emerson had to go on any training mission the regular troops did. But separate from the rest. So he went into the rifle range one day, and of course all the white soldiers were issued standard rifles. He wasn't. They were issued live ammunition. He wasn't.

"He was issued a wooden gun, and he had to get on the firing line, just like the others, and they told him that when the order comes to fire, you point your wooden gun, and you say, 'bang.'"

The Red Tail

Warren sang. Chester cooked. Wee fired a wooden gun. There were no great war heroes in the immediate family. Harry and Sam left and came back without encountering the enemy. Chester encountered an enemy of a different sort.

For the most part, black troops were kept out of action, but some fought, including the 761st Tank Battalion. General George Patton requested them for his Third Army and they fought in the famous Battle of the Bulge. Before their first battle, Patton gave them a speech.

"Men, you're the first Negro tankers to ever fight in the American Army. I would never have asked for you if you weren't good. I have nothing but the best in my Army. I don't care what color you are as long as you go up there and kill those Kraut sons of bitches.

"Everyone has their eyes on you and is expecting great things from you. Most of all, your race is looking forward to your success. Don't let them down and damn you, don't let me down!"

After the war in his book, *War As I Knew It*, Patton wrote, "Individually they were good soldiers, but I expressed my belief at the time, and have never found the necessity of changing it, that a colored soldier cannot think fast enough to fight in armor."

It was also believed that a colored soldier couldn't think fast enough to fight in the air. This wasn't just prejudice, it was science. In 1925, the U.S. Army War College performed a study and concluded that blacks were "incapable of flying airplanes."

The study says: "In the process of evolution the American negro has not progressed as far as the other subspecies of the human family...

"It is generally recognized that the pure blood American negro is inferior to our white population in mental capacity...The cranial cavity of the negro is smaller than the white; his brain weighing 35 ounces contrasted with 45 for the white.

"All officers, without exception, agree that the Negro lacks initiative, displays little or no leadership, and cannot accept responsibility. Some point out that these defects are greater in the Southern Negro...

"Due to his susceptibility to 'Crowd Psychology' a large mass of negroes, e.g., a division, is very subject to panic...An opinion held in common by practically all officers is that the negro is a rank coward in the dark. His fear of the unknown and unseen will prevent him from ever operating as an individual scout with success. His lack of veracity causes unsatisfactory reports to be rendered, particularly on patrol duty...

"On account of the inherent weaknesses in negro character, especially general lack of intelligence and initiative, it requires much longer time of preliminary training to bring a negro organization up to the point of training where it is fit for combat, than it does in the case of white men. All theoretical training is beyond the grasp of the negro—it must be intensely practical, supplemented by plain talks explaining the reasons for things in simple terms…"

But eventually the army established a training base at Tuskegee, Alabama, and after putting the trainees through rigorous training that bordered on torture, subjecting them to large, but fairly standard doses of racial humiliation, and begrudgingly acceding to the wishes of Eleanor Roosevelt, the army allowed these men to meet the German master race in the sky, man to man, machine to machine, small-cranium to large-cranium.

They were known as the Red Tails, because they painted the rear of their fighters red. Barely known during the war, they're now the famed Tuskegee Airmen, and they performed brilliantly.

Of the 992 pilots trained, 355 went to war and 84 died, 68 of them killed in action.

Collectively, they flew 1578 combat missions and 179 escort missions for bombers. It was once said they never lost a bomber, but that wasn't true. They lost bombers on seven missions, but that was very good. They destroyed some 260 enemy aircraft, damaged another 148 and destroyed more than 600 railcars. They even took out a destroyer.

Many stayed in the military for years. One who stayed was a fighter pilot born in 1920, the same year as Warren. He died in 2008. He flew more than 130 combat missions over Italy, France, and Germany. He started and ran the

Air ROTC programs at both Howard University and Tennessee State and retired as a lieutenant colonel.

He was Howard Baugh from Petersburg, Virginia, and he was Carolyn's brother.

Leaving Home

It was a new world. Hitler was dead. Japan was desolate, their empire ruined, their military vanquished. We'd avenged Pearl Harbor with ships and marines and flamethrowers and thousands of dead Japanese. We'd avenged Pearl Harbor by firebombing Tokyo and dropping two bombs that eliminated two cities. Tokyo lay in ruins. Hiroshima had vanished. Nagasaki had vanished. Each in a moment.

In Europe, the camps, the ovens, the piles of bodies, the tables full of rings and gold and teeth and hair, cut, extracted, and ripped from dead Jews, were discovered, the extermination of the Jews exposed.

Paris was spared, London and Liverpool heavily damaged. Stalingrad was rubble. Dresden was rubble. The Russians had ransacked, occupied, and raped Berlin in a very literal sense.

Banking systems, transportation systems, economies, and farmland were all ruined. There was starvation and famine, destruction, heartbreak, and disease. The soldiers came home. Or didn't. Or came home only to be buried.

Berlin was divided into four zones, American, British, Soviet, and French. The alliance of convenience between the United States, its allies, and the Soviet Union fell apart, and in 1948, Stalin formed a blockade to force the allies out of Berlin.

Instead, the allies flew right over the blockade and fed their troops and the two million citizens of free Berlin with two million tons of food, fuel, and supplies before the Soviets finally gave in, and the threat of an immediate third world war subsided.

We instituted the Marshall Plan to help free Europe rejuvenate itself. We created NATO to help free Europe protect itself.

In 1961, East Germany surrounded West Berlin with an ugly wall and called it the "Anti-Fascist Protection Rampart," claiming it would protect the glories of Soviet socialism and keep West German fascists out. But fascism was dead. West Germans did not want in to East Berlin, but thousands of East Berliners wanted out, and many would die trying to escape.

The United States was now the most powerful nation in the world and would assume the role of democracy's great protector, except in the South, where a perverted form of pseudo-democracy would prevail, and blacks would be oppressed, abused, and murdered with state-sanctioned impunity for another 20 years.

Soon the Soviet Union would explode an H-bomb, launch a satellite, bring Poland, Czechoslovakia, Romania, Bulgaria, Hungary, Albania, and East Germany firmly under control and form massive armies and the Warsaw Pact to confront NATO.

They would develop nuclear weapons and missiles, an arsenal powerful enough to annihilate the entire free world in less than a day, and perhaps would have used it, too, except they couldn't destroy us without destroying themselves. It was called mutually assured destruction. MAD. It was. Yet it prevented humanity from incinerating itself.

There would be a long Cold War. And although the U.S. and Russians would never meet on the field of battle or launch missiles from silos and subs or drop nuclear bombs on one another from planes, there would be plenty of battle by proxy, and another 90,000 American men would die in Korea and Vietnam, as the human race spent the next 45 years at the edge of extinction.

Back in Sykesville, the young men and women trickled home. Up Oklahoma Hill, the Dorsey boys were all gone, the chicken coops empty, the fields grown over and abandoned, and whatever grand plans Ed might have envisioned long ago, locked in his mind.

There would be no more great potato harvests, no more horses pulling plows, no more gutting pigs, no more slitting the throats of young roosters or sending crates of eggs to Henryton, no more Dorsey boys sleeping three to a bed, then sweating in the summer sun behind Frank the genius horse. The youngest threesome, Chester, Warren, and Emerson had all gone off to war. For Warren and Emerson it had been easy. For Chester it had been a nightmare.

Warren's career as a singing drill sergeant was over. His life on military bases had only just begun. His scholarship was gone. To get it back, he'd have to go through the whole process from the start. He decided not to. He would never become the next George Washington Carver.

It was disappointing, but only mildly so. He says, "Whatever life throws at you, you learn to take it and go with it."

He decided maybe he'd go into teaching and prove something to that old farmer. Wiley H. Bates High School in Annapolis offered an interview, but when he learned it paid $2200 a year, he decided to skip it. Instead, he put aside his degree in biology and his dreams of pursuing a doctorate and developing microorganisms to help poor farmers.

He went back to making boxes for cigarette cartons like Camels and Chesterfields and Lucky Strikes in that big old box factory half a mile southeast of Ellicott City on the Patapsco River. It was manual labor, but there was a skill to it, and if you were good, you could earn bonuses and make good money, and that's what he did, because when the war ended, he had a degree, but he sure didn't have any money.

Emerson traded in his wooden rifle and married a girl named Ethel Harris he met in college and followed home to Frederick. Fort Detrick was right outside the city, and he landed a job there. Emerson had a degree in agriculture, and at Detrick they were growing things, so they could figure out how to kill them.

In fact, the army was doing a lot at Detrick well suited to someone with Warren's background, someone who knew how to stare through a microscope and identify the little squiggling things staring back at him. They were working with microorganisms, or in common terminology, germs, but not so they could improve soil or cure disease. This was the army, and the army saw germs as potential weapons.

Warren got an interview. All he had to do was get there from Sykesville. He didn't have a car, so he decided to hitchhike the 25 miles to Frederick for his interview.

He walked six miles before catching a ride and getting off in Frederick about half an hour later. He got a job that day. He quit the box factory and started on Monday, the first day of August 1946.

A woman named Genevieve Holland rented him a bedroom on the second floor of a big place in the small part of town where they let black people live, and for six dollars a week he was in. He'd escaped Sykesville, Baltimore, Camp Lee, and had a new home now, or at least a room, in Frederick, Maryland.

Carolyn was teaching school in Petersburg, living with her parents in her nice home, and on September 7, 1946, in that nice home in Petersburg, Warren and Carolyn were married. It was a small wedding, maybe 25 or 30 people, mostly Carolyn's family. Howard couldn't make it. He was still in Italy with the military.

They married on a Saturday, then traveled back to Thelma's place in Baltimore. A woman across the street was away for a bit and she let them use her house for a one-night honeymoon. Then it was back to Frederick on Sunday night to their new home.

Only this time he didn't walk, he didn't hitchhike, he didn't doubt himself, and he would never be poor again. He got in the car with Carolyn, and off they went to Frederick and a whole new life together, with Chester Dorsey behind the wheel.

Carolyn Baugh, 24, in 1946, shortly before the wedding in
Petersburg.

Warren at 25. He and Carolyn went to the studio together.

Back row (left to right): Chester, Russell, Rosie, Everett, Vernon

Middle row: Clifton, Romulus, Mae, Catherine, Emerson

Front row: Thelma, Ed, Carrie, Warren

Above: Corporal Dorsey during the war.

OF THE COLORED PERSUASION

Whatever Chester had, it didn't kill him, just like the truck that fell on him didn't kill him. Minnie's telegram from the officials who break bad news said her husband was very ill and unlikely to survive. But they were wrong. An army doctor declared Chester so close to dead, he could hear the wings of angels flapping. Chester'd heard those wings before, and one more time, the angels flew off without him.

The army classified him 50 percent disabled and let him out. His recovery was slow. He returned to the box factory. When the workers went on strike and he couldn't afford it, he went to Springfield as a cook and worked there till he retired.

Chester took Warren and Carolyn out of Sykesville for good. Then he came home and lived the rest of his 87 years on Oklahoma Hill in the green house with Warren's prom date, where he would postpone his date with the angels till 2005.

Genevieve bumped the rent to $8 when Carolyn moved in. For that they got their one room. They got to use the kitchen. They got to share the bathroom with four or five other tenants. They got an address. They got a little radio and a new life.

Carolyn was not certified to teach in Maryland. So she was home in the room all day. She made her own clothes, she crocheted, she knitted Warren a sweater.

Warren made just less than $3,000 a year. They didn't get their first car, a 1935 Chevy, till 1951. It was all they could afford, but by 1955, they were doing well enough to buy a new Chevrolet.

There was a church across the street. The lady who owned the house belonged and so did Emerson and Ethel, so Warren and Carolyn joined, too.

Frederick had a small black population clustered on three streets. Warren and Carolyn didn't know much about the city, but now it was their home, and they started singing.

"Soon after we came to Frederick, when Carolyn was 24 or 25, she took voice lessons with a white guy who was the music minister for one of the local white congregations. And he suggested maybe she should audition in New York and go into the concert circuit."

But Carolyn wasn't really interested, and Warren wasn't too crazy about the idea either, so she stayed in Frederick and they sang together.

Another microbiologist at Detrick, a white guy named Thorn, invited them to join a community chorus. And they did. They were the first members who weren't white.

Somewhere around 1949, on Thorn's recommendation, they were invited to join the Frederick Community Chorus that practiced at Hood College. The director got in touch somehow, probably by phone, and invited them to rehearsal. Thorn hadn't mentioned the Dorseys' skin color. Somehow the man found out before their meeting and asked if he could visit their house and talk.

When they let him in, he apologized. He wanted to save them the embarrassment of coming to rehearsal. He told them the community chorus did not accept black people.

In 1947, Jackie Robinson broke into the majors with Brooklyn. He made a deal with Branch Rickey, the man who owned the team. For three years, he'd take whatever they threw at him, swallow his pride, and play. He wouldn't complain. He wouldn't retaliate. He would not fight. He would just play.

When the manager of the Phillies stood on the dugout steps and shouted at him, "Hey nigger. Hey nigger, nigger, nigger," when town after town, game after game, people called him names, sent him hate mail, threatened his life, threatened his family, Robinson kept his mouth shut and played, and the formerly hapless Dodgers won six National League pennants.

Warren never had to put up with anything like that. He'd spent most of his life isolated from white people, not abused by them. But like Robinson with Rickey, he had a deal with Carrie. It wasn't in words. It was just an understanding. He would work through the system. He would excel.

Maryland was a segregated state. That was reality. Warren wasn't going to make a big stink about singing with some people that didn't want him.

"We weren't looking for a fight," he says. "We just wanted to sing."

But quietly, he simmered.

"The first time we went to a movie in Frederick, the gallery that permitted African Americans was way over the rest of the theater. The only access was by steps on the outside. You had to climb these steps and then sit in this segregated balcony. We went once, and I vowed never to go again.

"The same sort of practice was true in the stores. The main clothing store didn't allow African Americans to try on clothes. You could buy them, but you couldn't try them on."

And, of course, the housing market was rigged.

"I started exploring finding another place, and got the idea to talk to a real estate agent. There were only white real estate agents, and I went to an agency. The name was Miller. Because I am so fair-skinned, he didn't know quite how to approach me. He didn't want to insult a possible customer, but he didn't have any intention of dealing with an African American, either.

"So he was showing me properties, and he hesitated and kept looking at me, and then he said, 'What is your nationality?' I told him I was an American. He pondered and he finally came out with it and said, 'I just have to ask you, are you of the colored persuasion?'

"I told him the truth. And then he had no properties to show me."

Umbrellas on the Toilet

For two and a half years they had one room, and shared a kitchen and a bathroom, but now Carolyn was expecting, and Warren wanted a better place. Eventually he came across a wreck in the part of town where they let people of the colored persuasion buy property.

The wreck had six small rooms and no bathroom. It had a flush toilet on the back porch with great advantages. There was fresh air. You didn't have to share it. It had a roof. It was enclosed, just not all that well, and when it rained you put up an umbrella.

The place was $3600, a year's salary, and just a bit more than Ed Dorsey paid for his farm, his house, and 40 acres in Sykesville. They had $1000 in the bank. They borrowed the rest. And for Warren a new career, of sorts, was born. He was going to teach himself home repair, as he and Emerson set out to renovate the wreck.

First they got rid of the rats. Then they fixed the bedroom, fixed the kitchen, and left the toilet on the porch. Warren found a furnace somewhere, put it in the basement, cut a hole through the floor, added a single register to pump heat upstairs, and for the first time, he owned a home with electricity, running water, an ultramodern heating system, and a flush toilet.

They moved in just in time to put up a tree and celebrate Christmas 1948.

Germ Warfare

Despite his degree, Warren started at Detrick with the title of lab technician, but he was soon promoted to microbiologist. He had a top-secret clearance. He wore goggles, white gloves, and protective suits. He stared into microscopes.

His focus was taking small deadly things and manufacturing them in large quantities so they could be dispersed to mass deadly effect. He worked with anthrax, bacterial molds, viruses, rickettsia, botulism. They weren't inventing anything. They were trying to harness something old, or in military parlance, weaponize nature.

He says, "Our job was to take these organisms and produce them not just in flasks but in gallon quantities, and even up into hundreds of gallon quantities, and still maintain the purity of the cultures."

It was complicated and risky. At least one man died while Warren was there. Warren himself breathed in something loose in the dangerous air and landed in the hospital for a couple weeks with symptoms like pneumonia.

But mostly he did fine. Soon enough he ran his own lab with a team of technicians under him. He helped write articles. He developed a new technique and patented it. And he became a father.

Two Sons

In 1948, if you were black in Frederick and having a baby, none of the local hospitals let you in. There was a nearby home for the aged with what Warren calls "a small birthing annex," and that's where the local black women had their babies.

There was a nurse in charge. You could bring your doctor. If you didn't have one and there was a problem, they'd call one over from the hospital. They found a nice man named Ed Thomas, a white doctor, who saw Carolyn a few times before the birth. He charged $2 an office visit and $45 for maternity cases.

Both the pregnancy and the birth went well, and with Doctor Thomas in attendance, Glenn Dorsey was born March 12, 1949. Warren was 28. Carolyn was 27. They brought home their baby on a bright sunny day. Spring came early that year, and Warren had a small garden in his small yard, and in the garden, waiting to greet their new baby, was a beautiful forsythia bush in full yellow bloom.

They had a kitchen, a bedroom, a bathroom, a baby, a hole in the floor where heat came up. The walls were painted. The house was clean. And they had the book.

"This was before Doctor Spock," Warren says. "I don't know who wrote the book, but the book said babies would sleep 22 hours a day and be awake about two to four during the day. Glenn slept for two to four hours during the day and was awake the other 20. We were frustrated. We were six months into raising this baby. During the periods he was crying, he was robbing everybody of sleep, and Carolyn and I had to take turns, especially at night, getting up with that boy.

"Then I discovered that if I sang to him, he would quiet down and look at me just as attentively as anybody could. I didn't sing children's songs, I sang songs. The one I sang most was 'South of the Border.' It was popular on the radio, and he would shut up and listen."

As Glenn became more alert, they began reading to him. Carolyn read children's books. Warren read texts on microbiology. There were no other kids in the neighborhood, and since Glenn had no playmates except his parents, he made up a collection of imaginary friends who lived in imaginary places.

There was no kindergarten in the school system, but the community operated a kindergarten in one of the public housing areas. They needed a teacher, and Carolyn became the teacher at the Esther E. Grinnage Kindergarten for $7 a week.

By then Glenn was three. Carolyn took him to school, and he finally met other kids. They were all older than him, and he got along just fine.

Warren says, "We often said Glenn grew up as an old man while he was still a kid. And really, he sort of acted that way."

They had a baby now and no extra money, and Warren got an idea.

"If my brother and I could buy property that was sort of rundown and fix it up like we did my place, we could do another property and maybe rent it out. And we were able to buy a house on the same street and convert it into two apartments. Later we got another and rented that out, too.

"That's how I supplemented my income and put a few dollars aside for some future venture or educating my kids. Sometimes I'd put in another eight hours at night working on properties with Emerson."

Rob was born March 13, 1954, the day after Glenn turned five. Unlike Glenn, Rob slept by the book. He ate, smiled, and paid attention. He was fascinated with numbers. He learned to count by going through a dictionary with 2006 pages. He went page by page, counting out loud to 2006, and then starting over.

He learned every state in the Union by three. He recognized them by shape from a jigsaw puzzle. He learned every county in Maryland. He learned their populations. Then he learned New York. He read from the encyclopedia. By the time he started school, he'd been reading proficiently for quite a while and was way ahead of the other first graders.

Top: Baby Glenn on a Christmas card.
Bottom: Young Rob (left) at the piano and Susan.

The Back of the Bus

In 1954, Maryland, Delaware, D.C., Kansas, and every former Confederate state of America still segregated schools by race, but on May 17 of that year, just two months after the birth of Rob Dorsey, in the case of *Brown v. Board of Education of Topeka*, the United States Supreme Court ruled that the legal separation of the Kansas school system was unconstitutional.

A year later they passed another ruling stating that across the nation, all schools must be desegregated "with all deliberate speed."

In 1955, the Brooklyn Dodgers won their only World Series, taking the Yankees in seven. By then Jackie Robinson was 36, did not have a good season, and was near the end of his career.

That August, just before the Dodgers won the Series, a Chicago boy visiting relatives in Money, Mississippi, and unfamiliar with the local culture, went into a grocery to buy some bubble gum. Carolyn Bryant, the woman who ran the store, accused him of some sort of inappropriate behavior. Six decades later, in 2017, she would admit that she'd mostly lied about the incident, but that was far too late to do Emmett Till any good.

Four days after Till entered that store, the woman's husband and his half-brother abducted the boy, beat him senseless, shot him in the head, wrapped a heavy fan around his neck with barbed wire, and tossed him in the Tallahatchie River.

He was 14. His name was Emmett Till. Three days after the murder, when someone pulled him out of the river, they discovered a face bludgeoned beyond recognition.

His mother held the funeral with the casket open so the world could see how her son came home from Mississippi.

She said, "Somebody is going to pay for this. The entire state of Mississippi is going to pay for this. I can't work. I have nothing left to work for. My whole life is ruined."

But she was wrong. Her life may have been ruined, but no one would pay for her son's murder, except *Look Magazine*. The killers were Roy Bryant and J.W. Milam. They were tried in Sumner, Mississippi. There was a black witness, a white jury, a dead boy, and no other suspects. The jury was all male. They deliberated 67 minutes and found the men not guilty.

A few months later, the murderers confessed. They described the crime to *Look*. Since you couldn't be tried twice for the same crime, Bryant and Milam made $4000 for torturing a kid, tossing him in a river, and selling the story to a magazine. It was the third lynching in Mississippi that year.

That December, 100 days after the murder of Emmett Till, 42-year-old Rosa Parks got on a bus in Montgomery, Alabama. She sat near the middle. The bus filled. A white man got on. There were four blacks sitting right behind the white section, and when the man got on, the driver told the blacks to move back so the man could sit.

Three got up. Rosa Parks didn't. It was a sudden decision that shouldn't have been all that dramatic. But this was Alabama. They arrested her.

The local blacks boycotted the Montgomery transportation system. A young preacher named Martin Luther King, Jr., arrived and addressed a crowd shortly after the arrest. He said, "You know, my friends, there comes a time when people get tired of being trampled over by the iron feet of oppression."

King was 26. In 13 years he'd be one of the most respected men in the world. He'd have a Nobel Prize for Peace and he'd be dead. But now he was young and new and inspiring. He taught non-violent resistance. And together with his friend and close ally, Ralph Abernathy, a World War II veteran and ordained minister, they organized the boycott of Montgomery's bus system.

Instead of riding the buses, the blacks of Montgomery used taxis and carpools and bikes. They walked. They rode mules and buggies pulled by horses. Black taxi drivers cut their fares.

Boycotters were attacked. Abernathy's home and church were both bombed. King's home was also bombed, with his wife and daughter inside. The bomb damaged the house and blew out all the windows. King's wife, Coretta, and their young daughter escaped unharmed.

The boycott lasted 381 days. The boycotters won. Ninety years after the Civil War, blacks in Alabama were no longer forced to sit in the back of the bus. But they couldn't vote.

Maryland Desegregates

Glenn finished his six years of elementary in an all-black school. During third grade, the school caught fire. Rather than mix them with white kids, they moved the black kids and some desks into makeshift classrooms in the warehouse of a feed company, and Glenn learned math and science and history where they used to store feed for chickens.

Frederick began desegregating in 1956. Glenn took his first classes with white kids in seventh grade at West Frederick Junior High in 1961. When he started, only the seventh grade was integrated. There were more than 400 students in the school, about 25 black.

All the teachers were white and most had never taught black kids before. Some accepted the new kids. Others insisted they didn't know how to teach them and didn't want to. Others were well intentioned and clueless. During his junior year, someone asked Glenn's teacher why black kids came in different shades. The teacher offered up an explanation involving the hot African climate and the gradual adaption of the black race to differing weather conditions.

Warren says, "I think there's a more logical explanation."

He also says that though Maryland's schools were de-segregated, they weren't actually integrated, explaining it this way.

"Desegregation means legal barriers to accessing schools, public accommodations, and all the other elements of separation are removed. Integration means you are fully accepted with an equal chance of participation.

"That didn't happen early on. Legal barriers were removed. The quality of educational material was no longer inferior for African-American kids. They were exposed to the same learning materials and same level of instruction as everyone else. But were all the children fully accepted? Not by any means, and I don't know if they have been yet."

By the time Glenn entered Frederick High, the novelty of mixed-race schools had worn off. He excelled. He was typically grouped with all white kids and made a number of white friends.

A cousin in Baltimore introduced him to ham radio. He learned Morse code. He set up an amateur radio operation in his basement and talked to people around the world.

Other than those weeks in the grain warehouse, Glenn had few problems going to school in Frederick. He was lucky.

Little Rock

Deeper South, desegregating with "all deliberate speed" meant never. In Congress, 101 members including 97

Southern Democrats issued a manifesto. They called it The Declaration of Constitutional Principles, accused the Supreme Court of "clear abuse of judicial power," and stated their intention to overturn the court's decision to integrate the schools.

The manifesto stated: "This unwarranted exercise of power by the Court, contrary to the Constitution, is creating chaos and confusion in the States principally affected. It is destroying the amicable relations between the white and Negro races that have been created through 90 years of patient effort by the good people of both races. It has planted hatred and suspicion where there has been heretofore friendship and understanding."

That friendship and understanding were on full display in Little Rock, Arkansas not long after. In 1957, most southern schools were still segregated by race. That September, a Federal Court ordered the desegregation of Central High in Little Rock. Governor Orval Faubus sent in the Arkansas National Guard to make sure it didn't happen. Two thousand guardsmen surrounded the school.

There's a famous picture of a black girl in sunglasses in a white pleated skirt with a book pressed under her arm, walking alone away from the school on September 4, 1957.

Behind the black girl is another girl with a wide-open mouth. The white girl with the wide-open mouth is shouting at the black girl. Her name is Hazel Bryan, and according to some accounts, she's saying something along the lines of this.

"Go home, nigger! Go back to Africa!"

The black girl in the sunglasses is Elizabeth Eckford. She's 15. She was supposed to enter the school through a different entrance with eight other black kids, but her family had no phone, and when plans changed, no one told her. She was on her own with a couple hundred angry white people trailing behind her. She was terrified. When she turned to an older white woman for help, the woman spat in her face.

High school kids chanted. "Two, four, six, eight, we don't want to integrate." Others shouted, "Lynch her."

She made it to the bus stop, where she cried and couldn't stop. News photographers formed a barrier around her. A white woman protected her. Elizabeth's father was out looking for her with his revolver and his three bullets. Eventually she got on a bus and rode away into her mother's arms and history.

The picture made her famous. It exposed the federal government and President Eisenhower as weak and insufficiently willing to impose the law. Shortly after seeing the pictures, the smiling, apolitical Louis Armstrong said, "The way they are treating my people in the South, the government can go to hell." He called President Eisenhower two-faced. He called Governor Faubus a "no good mother-fucker."

Eisenhower ordered the 101st Airborne into Arkansas. They were known as the "Screaming Eagles." They'd once parachuted into hostile territory during D-Day to help liberate France from Nazi rule. Now they stood guard in Arkansas so nine black kids could go to high school.

Elizabeth made it through the year. Her fellow students made it a hard one. Glenn Dorsey put up with a few months in a feed warehouse. Elizabeth Eckford was shoved, kicked, punched, pushed down stairs, knocked on her face, spit at, spit on, and serenaded in the gym with racist lyrics. They hit her with eggs and tomatoes, spitballs and sharpened pencils. They threw soda bottles at her and snowballs filled with rocks.

In 1958, the military went home. Rather than integrate them, the people of Arkansas voted to close all the state's public high schools. No one went to high school that year. Elizabeth moved on, attended other schools, attended college, served in the military, and failed several times to kill herself.

ALL HELL

In 1957, the Dodgers traded Jackie Robinson to the New York Giants. Robinson retired instead. In Georgia, a state senator named Leon Butts presented a bill excluding blacks from playing baseball with whites. The Georgia Senate approved it.

The Soviets launched Sputnik on October 4th, a tiny satellite that shocked the world, and Warren's family moved again, this time to a lot set aside for African Americans on an old apple orchard. They built a house on the orchard for $14,000 and have been there ever since. Today the house is long paid off and worth a quarter-million dollars.

Not long after Warren, Carolyn, and the boys moved into their new home in Maryland, 120 miles south of them in the state next door, in the hill country of Caroline County, Virginia, a sheriff and two deputies broke down the door and walked into the bedroom of Richard and Mildred Loving. It was 2 a.m., July 11, 1958. The law officers carried flashlights and guns.

The Lovings were uneducated rural Virginians. They were an ordinary married couple who loved one another. Except Mildred was black and Richard was white. The Lovings had recently married in D.C. The sheriff broke into their house and arrested them for defying Virginia's Racial Integrity Act of 1924.

The year Warren and Carolyn moved into their new place, marriage between blacks and whites was illegal in Virginia and 24 other states. The Lovings were sentenced to one year in prison for "cohabiting as man and wife, against the peace and dignity of the Commonwealth."

Leon M. Bazile, the judge who did the sentencing, wrote:

"Almighty God created the races white, black, yellow, malay and red, and he placed them on separate continents. And but for the interference with his arrangement there would be no cause for such marriages. The fact that he separated the races shows that he did not intend for the races to mix."

The Lovings served no time. They were banned for 25 years from the hills of Virginia where they'd grown up.

Back in Maryland, on May 13, 1960, Carolyn gave birth to her only daughter. She was born in the actual maternity ward of Frederick Memorial Hospital, and they named her Susan. Warren still gets excited remembering his first look.

"In the nursery with the other children, Susan looked like she was about six months ahead. She weighed over 10 pounds. She was as large as about three babies."

By 1960, Frederick Memorial no longer had one small ward set aside for blacks. Black women could give birth inside the hospital with white women, and Susan was born into a time where, outside the South, black Americans were moving closer to the mainstream of American life, particularly in sports and entertainment, but in politics, too. And they were doing great and amazing things.

In 1959, with John Coltrane on sax, trumpeter Miles Davis recorded *Kind of Blue*, the greatest selling record in the history of jazz. In 1962, with the NBA's Philadelphia Warriors, Wilt Chamberlain scored 100 points in a single game.

There was Chuck Berry and Little Richard and Motown, and in 1963, Sidney Poitier became the first black to win an Oscar. In 1966, the Braves moved from Milwaukee to Atlanta, Georgia, where eight years earlier Leon Butts had presented his bill barring blacks from playing baseball with whites, and where the Braves' Hank Aaron would eventually hit more than 300 of his 755 homers on his way to surpassing Babe Ruth's old record for career home runs.

In 1967, Thurgood Marshall of Baltimore became the first black Supreme Court Justice. In Massachusetts, Edward Brooke became the first black Senator of the twentieth century. In 1968, Shirley Chisholm became the first black woman elected to congress, and Arthur Ashe became the first black to win the U.S. Open in tennis.

For Warren's young family, insulated and safe in Frederick, the sixties were a fairly calm time. For Susan, young and friendly, pretty and talented, they were happy years.

When she was little, as soon as she was strong enough to hang on and ride, every night for years, Susan rode up to bed on her father's back. He got down on all fours. He kicked and bucked and neighed. He crawled and galloped, and Susan hung on and laughed until he flipped her into bed.

Twice a week, Tuesdays and Fridays, he took her shopping with him at the A&P. When he worked around the house with his screwdrivers and wrenches and hammers and nails, Susan was his assistant.

Susan eventually got too old to ride his back to bed. She grew up and acted and danced, sang, played the flute, and did great on stage and in school.

Carolyn gave piano lessons to the neighborhood kids, conducted recitals in the house, and ruined her voice hollering at first graders. Glenn and Rob both excelled, but they struggled, too, in ways their parents didn't really understand.

Warren thrived at Fort Detrick. Life was good for the Dorseys in Maryland.

But in the deeper South and the country at large, all hell broke loose. There were marches and sit-ins, Freedom Rides, bombings, assassinations, and war.

In Birmingham, Alabama, in May 1963, during the famous Children's Crusade, firemen blasted skinny schoolchildren with powerful hoses. Police went after them with dogs. Hundreds were arrested and hauled away in school buses and paddy wagons. Photos and news clips of the dogs and the clubs and the soaked children pinned to brick walls by jets of water shocked the world.

On June 11, 1963, when James Hood and Vivian Malone tried to enter the University of Alabama, Governor George Wallace, surrounded by Alabama State Troopers, met Hood and Malone at the entrance to Foster Auditorium, and refused to let the black students enter the school.

Earlier in the year, he'd made a heroic pronouncement:

"From this day, we are standing up, and the heel of tyranny does not fit the neck of an upright man. Let us rise to the call of freedom-loving blood that is in us, and send our answer to the tyranny that clanks its chains upon the South. In the name of the greatest people that have ever trod this earth, I draw a line in the dust and toss the gauntlet before the feet of tyranny, and I say, segregation now, segregation tomorrow and segregation forever."

So Wallace took his stand against tyranny. He stood with armed men in the door of a school to stop two black kids from stepping inside. President John Kennedy federalized the Alabama National Guard. They no longer reported to Wallace, they reported to him and forced Wallace aside.

That night Kennedy spoke to America.

"This afternoon the presence of Alabama National Guardsmen was required on the University of Alabama to carry out the final and unequivocal order of the United States District Court of the Northern District of Alabama. That order called for the admission of two clearly qualified young Alabama residents who happened to have been born Negro. That they were admitted peacefully on the campus is due in good measure to the conduct of the students of the University of Alabama, who met their responsibilities in a constructive way.

"I hope that every American, regardless of where he lives, will stop and examine his conscience about this and other related incidents. This Nation was founded by men of many nations and backgrounds. It was founded on the principle that all men are created equal, and that the rights of every man are diminished when the rights of one man are threatened."

Several hours after the speech, a Klansman named Byron De La Beckwith shot Medgar Evers in the back as he stepped out of the car in his driveway in Jackson, Mississippi. Evers was 37 and a veteran of World War II. He was the NAACP field director of the South, and at the top of the Klan's hit list.

In his car were a bunch of NAACP T-shirts that said, "Jim Crow Must Go." He died in the hospital 50 minutes later.

Byron De La Beckwith was eventually convicted of murdering Evers. But not till 1994.

On August 28, 1963, in the shadow of the Lincoln Memorial, Carolyn's old choir mate Camilla Williams sang the National Anthem and Martin Luther King, Jr., stood before a massive crowd where, like Lincoln at Gettysburg and Kennedy the night De La Beckwith gunned down

Medgar Evers, a doomed man urged the nation to live up to that thing about all men being created equal.

"I have a dream that one day this nation will rise up and live out the true meaning of its creed: 'We hold these truths to be self-evident; that all men are created equal.' I have a dream that one day on the red hills of Georgia the sons of former slaves and the sons of former slave owners will be able to sit together at the table of brotherhood. I have a dream that one day even the state of Mississippi, a state sweltering with the heat of injustice, sweltering with the heat of oppression, will be transformed into an oasis of freedom and justice.

"I have a dream that little children will one day live in a nation where they will not be judged by the color of their skin but by the content of their character. I have a dream today.

"I have a dream that one day down in Alabama, with its vicious racists, with its governor having his lips dripping with the words of interposition and nullification, one day right there in Alabama little black boys and black girls will be able to join hands with little white boys and white girls as sisters and brothers. I have a dream today."

King spoke of his dream on August 28. On September 5, Governor George Wallace of Alabama expressed his own desires.

Wallace said, "The society is coming apart at the seams. What good is it doing to force these situations when white people nowhere in the South want integration? What this country needs is a few first-class funerals..."

Eleven days later, on Sunday, September 15, members of the United Klans of America stuck a box of dynamite under the steps of Birmingham's 16th Street Baptist Church and set a timer.

There were 400 people in the church, all black, 80 kids, when the church exploded. There were four girls in the bathroom. They were Denise McNair, Carole Robertson, Cynthia Wesley, and Addie Mae Collins, 11, 14, 14, and 14. All buried in the rubble.

King wired the President. He warned of "the worst racial holocaust this nation has ever seen."

He wired Wallace. "The blood of four little children...is on your hands."

Two months after Denise McNair, Carole Robertson, Cynthia Wesley, and Addie Mae Collins died in the bathroom of their church, John Kennedy drove into the city of Dallas in the formerly Confederate state of Texas. A few hours later, Lyndon Johnson was President of the United States, Jacqueline Kennedy was a widow, and the nation was treated to a first-class funeral.

A few months later, on July 2, 1964, President Johnson signed the Civil Rights Act of 1964. It ended discrimination in public places, demanded the integration of schools, and made employment discrimination illegal. On August 6, 1965, he signed the Voting Rights Act, removing state and local barriers that stopped blacks from voting.

In 1967, in the case of *Loving v. Virginia*, the Supreme Court invalidated all state laws prohibiting marriage between the races, and Richard and Mildred Loving were able to return home.

On March 31, 1968, drained by the bloody war in Vietnam, Johnson announced he would relinquish the presidency at the end of his term. Five days later, on April 4, Martin Luther King, Jr., stepped out onto a balcony of the Lorraine Motel in Memphis, Tennessee, where a single bullet crashed through his right cheek, broke his jaw, shattered a few vertebrae, and cut his jugular vein.

On April 9, George Wallace was treated to another first-class funeral. They loaded King's casket onto a farm wagon made of wood, and two mules pulled him more than three miles from Ebenezer Baptist Church to Morehouse College in Atlanta. Some 100,000 people lined the streets and watched mostly in silence, as slowly, the dead King rolled by.

Riots broke out in more than 100 cities. In D.C., there were fires and looting and violence. Johnson sent about 13,600 troops. Soldiers stood guard before the White House. Marines mounted machine guns on the steps of the Capitol. There were 12 deaths, more than 1000 injuries, more than 6000 arrests, more than 900 stores ruined, and whole blocks smashed to rubble.

It was as bad, or worse, in Baltimore, where martial law was imposed and Governor Agnew sent in thousands of National Guard and 500 Maryland State Police. When they proved insufficient, Johnson sent 5000 paratroopers and other federal troops from Fort Bragg in North Carolina. Baltimore was an occupied city with snipers and soldiers with fixed bayonets. Six died, hundreds were injured, thousands rounded up and arrested.

Warren watched it all on television from his home in Frederick. He was a middle-aged scientist with an eight-year-old daughter, two sons, and a secure life. He went to work each day. He sang in the choir. He played pinochle with a group of friends. He watched the Freedom Riders and lunch counter sitters, the little kids marching out of churches against fire hoses and dogs, with great admiration.

He watched the rioting, the looting, the violence, arson, and destruction with dread.

"I felt a tremendous loss. It wasn't just the King family that felt the loss. It was the whole African-American community. But any time you use violent ways of protest or violent ways of trying to achieve a goal, I consider that a mistake.

"I think King's was a much more sensible way of doing it, and in the long run, it probably was the only way we are going to achieve harmony between nations, between races, between governments. I think it's the only way."

SMART ENOUGH TO TEACH

Nearly half a century after King died his brutal death, and troops with guns and chemicals and bayonets occupied the city where Ed once hustled pool and Warren once sold tickets to Louis Armstrong concerts, in the much calmer days of 2014, Warren and Rosie came to the old schoolhouse in Sykesville to give their annual talk. It was a cold day with a freak snowstorm in the middle of spring, and the crowd was smaller than usual.

Mae, who would turn 95 that July, was away sick, and Rosie, normally a fabulous and effervescent speaker, silly and full of laughs, seemed more subdued than normal. She said she missed her sister.

Mae still lived in the same house on Lafayette Avenue in Northwest Baltimore that she'd moved to in the forties. She was several years older than Rosie, but they'd known each other more than 80 years, they'd both lived in Baltimore most of that time, and both lost their husbands in

1979, when neither was very old. And neither married again.

Warren, too, didn't talk as long as usual that day. He looked frailer than last time I saw him. Shortly he would get out the tiller and prepare his plot in Frederick for another season of digging and growing things. He would walk on his treadmill 15 minutes each day. He would mow the grass. It would grow back and he would mow it again. Just as he'd always done. Week after week. Year after year. Through his forties, fifties, sixties, seventies, eighties, nineties.

But he would also find himself on the floor one day and wonder how he got there. He would begin fainting often enough to get worried. He would become terribly exhausted after each brief bit of work, and would soon confront an operation to stabilize his weakened heart. Something was wrong in there.

But he spoke well that afternoon, if not long. He spoke indignantly of the 1857 Dred Scott decision, and the infamous opinion of Chief Justice Roger Taney that because Scott was black he possessed "no rights which the white man was bound to respect."

Referring to the most famous statement in the Declaration of Independence, that "all men are created equal," Taney wrote that "it is too clear for dispute, that the enslaved African race were not intended to be included, and formed no part of the people who framed and adopted this declaration."

After expressing his outrage at Taney, Warren held up something for the crowd. He called it his "prized possession." It was a framed piece of paper more than 40 years old.

Back in 1970, with Glenn in college, Rob in high school, and Susan still in grammar school, some 32 years after that farmer said, "Boy, you know a nigger ain't got sense enough to teach," Warren reached a turning point.

Six thousand Americans died that year in Vietnam. We invaded Cambodia, and in Ohio at Kent State University, the National Guard shot four protesting college students and left them dead on the ground.

Between 1965 and 1973, the United States dropped eight million tons of bombs on Vietnam, three times the tonnage dropped during WWII by all the combined powers. Some of those bombs included napalm, a mix of chemicals and gasoline that formed a superhot jelly and stuck to anything it touched, burned for nearly 10 minutes, and caused excruciating pain and almost certain death.

We also sprayed millions of tons of defoliants, including Agent Orange, to destroy forests and fields and devastate the food supplies of Vietnamese farmers in an effort to starve and flush out the Viet Cong Guerillas.

Use of Agent Orange ended in 1970. Use of napalm ended in 1972. But even compared to all that bombing, napalm, and Agent Orange, germ warfare was considered especially inhumane, and as President Nixon pushed the war, he cut back on research at Detrick.

Warren feared jobs at Detrick would soon dry up. He tried his luck at the National Institutes of Health in Bethesda. The interview went well, but coming home, somewhere in the frantic traffic on Route 270 between Bethesda and Frederick, he realized he couldn't do it.

He was 50. He didn't want to spend the next decade alternately inching along or flying at high speed down a crowded road filled with fumes and horns and crazy drivers in bad moods. He got lucky again. There were vacancies in the Maryland school system and trouble filling them. Goucher College in Baltimore was offering master's degrees to degreed people with no previous background in education.

Soon Warren was back in college for the first time in 25 years.

He says, "It was a high-intensity program. You went to school six days a week, sometimes at night, and you could qualify for a master's degree in a year."

And 44 years after entering that master's program at Goucher, while big heavy snowflakes coated the ground outside Sykesville's old colored schoolhouse, Warren held something up for the crowd.

He'd been his high school's valedictorian. He'd served in the military during the country's greatest war. He'd excelled at math and biology in college and finished second in his class. He'd published articles, received a patent, and risen from a barefoot farm boy to a mathematician and a microbiologist, but nothing he'd ever done meant as much to him as what he got from Goucher College in 1971.

It was a diploma, a master's in elementary education. It meant Warren could teach and that old farmer could go to hell.

"I felt vindicated," he says. "And not just for me, but for a lot of people. The attitude of that farmer—that he looked down on me—that people like him looked down on people of my race—I felt I had vindicated my whole race and my own daddy, too.

"That was his biggest problem. He could never deal with being put down all the time, when he knew he had the ability and could have performed at a much higher level than he was permitted to. I felt vindicated for him."

In 1971, he entered a classroom at Waverley Elementary School in Frederick and faced a room full of young white faces. A year later he transferred to East Frederick Elementary School. He taught fifth and sixth grade science and math. He loved it.

Two years later, he took an assistant principal job in a school with a single black student, in Middletown, not far from Frederick, and a year later became principal of Carroll Manor Elementary School in Adamstown in southeastern Frederick County.

There were 400 students. Warren added one black teacher, increasing the number of black teachers to one. The students were mostly white farm kids. He didn't care all that much about their color.

"My attitude was, I am blind to who you are, how you are dressed, where you come from, how you're groomed.

They come to school to learn, and it's my responsibility to provide the best opportunity I can on an equal basis to every kid.

"My first responsibility was the county's kids. My dedication was providing for these kids the best I could. Most were poor white kids. I didn't have any problems with the kids, but the parents were very critical, and I had to talk to the school board on more than one occasion.

"They gave me more grief because I was a black principal. In fact, when I was first assigned there, the secretary, an elderly white lady, said, 'Oh no, that's not going to work here. He's black.' But as long as I was there, she was respectful and supportive."

His worst problem was parents fighting over their kids. Sometimes literally. On one occasion, a husband and wife who were separated got into a fight outside school, swearing and swinging and wrestling in the grass.

There were other problems, but here's what bothered him most.

"It was typical to have three groups in each class. The kids in the lower group were the poor performing kids. Many of the teachers, who were predominately white, when they met their classes, almost automatically assigned their African-American kids to the lower group.

"You start out with kids in kindergarten and on the basis of testing, most of the kids are at similar levels, but because of the attitude of the teachers, you could gradually see these African-American kids continually recommended for the lower group and falling behind. By the time they reached middle school they had sort of copped out on school, and by the time they reached high school, many were in out-and-out rebellion."

It was an old problem and not one he would ever fix. In 1981, he decided it was over.

"I was 60. I'd been working at one thing or another or going to school all my life, and I thought it was time to take a break. I thought younger people with younger ideas and higher energy would be better suited to operating the school, and I wanted the younger ones to have that opportunity."

He retired. Carolyn had retired the year before. For 10 years they'd gone off every day and taught school. Now they were home with a long retirement ahead.

Warren set off to make his mother proud. That was his main goal. But there was something else driving him all those years. He wrote a story about it and sent it to me. Here's how the story ends. "Yes, Mr. Farmer, THIS NIGGER HAD SENSE ENOUGH TO TEACH."

The Spirit Leaving the Corpse

Back in Sykesville, after the Depression and the fire and the war, through the fifties and into the eighties, the town slowly died. All Frank Brown's cottages were either gone now or somehow converted into private homes, and just about no one ever heard of James Sykes, or his boring old mill and washed-out hotel. A couple thousand people still lived in town, but its best days were long gone.

In the sixties, Main Street was still busy. You could get a haircut. You could get your shopping done. There was a hardware store, where Santa came once a year. There was the Sykesville 5 & 10 and the Harris place.

There was A.C. Brown's Sykesville State Bank. There was Bernard McDougall's Pharmacy and Henry Forsythe's store. There was a barber named Happy Keeney, who kept pigeons in his shop and also served as mayor. There was a deaf fellow named Frenchie who rode a bike about town and carried a small monkey with him everywhere. There was a cop named Millard Cooper, who smoked cigars, kept the peace, plowed the snow, and collected the trash.

In 1957, the high school burned. In the sixties, the state re-routed Route 32, which once came straight through Main Street, directly past town, stranding Sykesville on the other side of the river, hidden behind trees, forgotten, mostly invisible, and of no importance to anyone who didn't live there.

When Warren and Mae walked Route 32 to school in the twenties and thirties, there wasn't much on it. Near the intersection of Routes 32 and 26, the gas station and convenience store hub of modern Eldersburg, there was an old country store, where they could wait out of the rain and the cold for the bus. And almost nothing else. An aerial photo from the thirties shows farmland in every direction around the naked intersection.

Now the road that once ran through Main Street skipped Sykesville altogether and took a direct line to Eldersburg. And as Eldersburg filled with strip malls and houses, Sykesville deteriorated from a small, self-sufficient place where you could walk downtown for anything you needed, to a different sort of small place, where everything depended on the car and getting out to Eldersburg, or further away to Westminster or Ellicott City or the planned city of Columbia, to acquire the basic necessities.

Once a place where people came to get what they needed, Sykesville became a place people left to get what they needed.

In 1986, Bob Allen wrote a long article about the town in the *Baltimore City Paper*.

He wrote, "Sykesville is like a slumbering little piece of the past. It is a rustic, if slightly decayed little town of 2400 people, mysteriously marooned in the sluggish backwaters of time."

To enter town from Route 32 on the Howard County side, you passed the Patapsco Inn and the Sykesville Inn, or some manifestation of the two, as they changed names frequently over the years. But they were always there, two boxy dives at the edge of town.

Once over the bridge, came the abandoned train station, and a few yards further, the McDonald block that burned in 1937 and the brick bank building that stopped the fire and saved the rest of town. By the late sixties, the old bank building housed a liquor store, and a noisy gang hung around out front.

Harry Sandosky, a local carpenter and former marine, who'd survived the American landing on Iwo Jima, and more or less held Sykesville together in those days, got so sick of the fighting and noise, he bought the building and closed the liquor store. But the drinking just moved under the bridge, where cans and bottles and butts and empty cigarette packs lay in the rocks and rolled and blew into the water.

Near the end of 1966, someone broke into McDougall's Pharmacy and stole $500 worth of cash and merchandise, including watches, transistor radios, and syringes. McDougall was Sykesville's mayor at the time.

They built a fire station on Main Street and it caught fire in 1969. Two trucks and most of the equipment were destroyed. One truck escaped, then stopped in the street and helped fight the fire. Eventually the fire station moved out of town, north up Route 32.

In 1972, a '60 Chevrolet and a '65 Bel Air were stolen on Main Street, and the *Herald* wrote, "Time was when you could safely leave your car unlocked in Sykesville. But apparently that day is gone."

That June, Hurricane Agnes came. As the endless rain poured, masses of rats fled town for higher ground on nearby farms. On June 22, the *Herald* reported that bridges were out, cables were down, trains were out, and all "rail traffic south from Philadelphia was cancelled due to area flooding."

And the bridge into Sykesville was gone. It was a scary thing, 90 years old, rickety and rattling, and now, as the *Herald* reported, it "lay in a heap several hundred feet downstream, barely recognizable."

For the next three years, Sykesville's Main Street ended at the banks of the Patapsco, with no way across without getting wet.

The post office moved off Main Street and then out of town completely and up to Eldersburg. The Harris Department Store shut down after 76 years, but Margaret Harris was long gone by then. She'd never married and passed away in 1955.

In 1981, the last freight train stopped at Sykesville's B&O station. In 1983, the *Herald* shut down.

Former Mayor Jon Herman, who moved to town in 1984, describes it this way.

"The town could have doubled for an abandoned old wild west set. You could imagine wind blowing dust and tumbleweed down Main Street. A *Baltimore Sun* reporter who visited wrote that there was a dog sleeping in the middle of Main Street. I later met this reporter, and he verified that this was true. There were no housing developments, just farms surrounding the historic town."

Mark Rychwalski, who moved in a year after Herman and later served as head of the town council, says, "It was a ghost town. It seemed frozen in time. A lot of days there wouldn't be a single car on Main Street. Nobody was around. Everything was closed. I remember thinking, what the hell is this place?"

In his 1986 article, Bob Allen wrote: "Even early on a Friday evening, Sykesville's Main Street already looks like they rolled up the sidewalks hours ago...there is little movement and almost no sign of life.

"The windows of the darkened storefronts seem to stare blankly out upon the solitude of the empty sidewalks and the narrow street. There is little or no traffic."

In the same article, Allen quotes former town manager James Schumacher: "When I was 18 or 19, I worked in a food market on Main Street. There were terrible problems with rats. They'd eat holes in the bags of dog food, and sometimes you could hear them scurrying around in the back."

But through all that, on the other side of the river, in Howard County, the bars lived on and thrived. By the eighties they were known as Suzie's and The Duke's Place.

In 1985, Howard County tried to shut down The Duke's Place. Allen wrote that undercover cops reported "drunken brawls and beatings (some of which ended in hospitalizations), firearms being discharged in the parking lot, illicit dice games, patrons so intoxicated that they were unable to walk.

"Also observed were persistent incidents of flagrant discrimination against blacks."

During one brawl, a man fired a shotgun into the air. Another was stabbed. Finally, in May 1986, Douglas Kennedy of Sykesville was shot and killed in the parking lot of Suzie's on a night when three fights inside the bar went unreported to police.

Lloyd Helt, a preacher's son from Pennsylvania who served as Sykesville's mayor from 1982 to 1994 and once referred to Eldersburg as "an abomination," summed the era up this way.

"Sykesville was sleeping for a long time and almost died. There was a point in the seventies when a lot of merchants who ran the town government were very depressed and negative. They just weren't making it economically. The town council was ready to turn the town charter over to the county and let them run it—to, in fact, dissolve the town. You might say the spirit was leaving the corpse."

The Hidden Hill

Up Oklahoma Hill, hidden away within the increasingly hidden town, in the parallel universe where the Dorseys lived, things were mostly quiet, and the decades rolled by with very little change. The Depression didn't change life much for people in Sykesville's black neighborhood. Neither did the war. The things rationed were mostly things black Sykesville did without anyway.

But it did get quieter up there. There were no more passenger trains, and the freight trains came by far less often and no longer stopped in Sykesville. The squawk and smell of chickens, the laughter of kids named Dorsey and Johnson and Green and Norris, the guitar of Wes Anderson, the powerful crack of Big Raymond's bat, the chatter of Gene Norris from behind the plate, "This batter's got a notion," had long ago faded away.

The town's attitudes toward its black residents probably hadn't changed all that much over the decades. People who've lived here a long time tell of a Sykesville mayor who opposed building a community swimming pool because, "There will be no way to keep the darkies out."

Into the sixties and probably beyond, blacks were not served in the two bars at the edge of town, but had to get their drinks outside through a rear window or door. In a Facebook group called "Sykesville and Eldersburg Back in the Day," a woman told this story of being fired by the owner of the Fire Bell restaurant on Main Street in the mid-sixties.

"She fired me because I served a milkshake to my black girlfriend, Faith Gaither, who came in with some white girlfriends and sat in the front booth together. When she saw what I had done, she stomped into the front of the restaurant from the kitchen. She forcefully grabbed the shade on the window of the front door and declared, 'We're closed.' My friends got up and left without a word to me."

Even as late as the seventies and possibly into the eighties, the Klan gathered and burned their crosses in Gamber, just a few miles north of Sykesville.

But in that private world up the hill, it probably didn't matter all that much. They lived the life they'd always led, except there were televisions now, and electric light, and sometime in the early forties, a man from the bank in Manchester came out for a visit. The man from the bank called the Dorsey's loan a "nuisance mortgage," and said they were trying to get rid of them. So he offered them a deal. Nine dollars a month for 10 years. Ed and Carrie took it, and by 1952, they'd paid off the mortgage.

They modernized a bit. They bought their first electric icebox. They bought a propane stove for the kitchen. They bought a television. But never a car.

They'd always lived simply. When the kids were young, they'd celebrated Easter by eating eggs, which was a luxury, because the rest of the year, eggs were money.

On Christmas they would bind evergreen branches with cord they saved from packages, and with branches and cord and wire, they built their own wreaths and covered all the windows downstairs.

Carrie collected coupons from the borax soap she used for her washing. With the coupons, she got each kid at least one toy, maybe a ball, a top, a game of tiddlywinks.

They cut down a Christmas tree from somewhere in their woods and put it in the living room. Each Christmas, Ed went into Baltimore and came back with a crate of oranges, bananas, and peanuts from a place called Jeppi. He gave the kids 50 cents each to buy gifts for each other.

Those days were long past, but still, the family got together often through the fifties and into the sixties, visiting each others' houses for various occasions, setting up tables around the house and everyone playing pinochle.

Emerson and Warren painted the roof of the old farmhouse, painted the walls, repaired the woodwork, rebuilt the chimneys. They added a bathroom in the late fifties, dug the whole thing out by hand and added a septic tank, and for the first time, Ed and Carrie had indoor plumbing, an indoor shower, and indoor toilet.

Ed got some social security. Thelma kept an eye on her parents and gave them what help she could. But time chipped away at the house and the fields and the family, and on March 12, 1953, the *Sykesville Herald* printed the following on page two under "News for Our Colored Readers."

March 12, 1953

Clifton Dorsey passed away Wednesday morning. He had been a patient in University Hospital for the past three weeks. He became extremely ill Tuesday morning after returning from work on the night before, and later was taken to the hospital where his condition remained critical.

He had been in a coma all during his stay there. An operation was performed upon his brain. Pneumonia set in twice, but on Friday, the doctors who previously had lost hope for his improvement, saw a slight change in his condition for the better. It was a most unusual case, one that could not be immediately determined even after the operation by specialists. Funeral arrangements have not been announced.

Clifton was born 16 years before Warren in 1904, the year Sykesville became a town and the family was still young and on the move and fresh out of Bush Park. He'd married Mr. Jim Norris's daughter Sarah in 1923 and bought a small house on Oklahoma Hill with four rooms and a small kitchen, and there he and Sarah raised 12 children.

Warren didn't really know him that well. By the time Warren started school, Clifton was already in his twenties. Clifton drank more hard liquor than was good for him, and Warren says, "Much of his life Clifton worked pick-up jobs and part-time if somebody wanted him. Harris used him a lot delivering groceries. But often he had very limited funds and was at his wit's end how to feed all those kids.

"We used to share some of the produce we grew with them. Those kids had a rough life. But Sarah never complained. She was always smiling. And those kids turned out to be excellent people."

Clifton was working steadily now at the box factory and had been for more than 10 years, when suddenly, at 49, he collapsed. It's possible his life might have gone differently if Ed had signed a piece of paper a long time ago.

"When Clifton was 14, Professor Lee tried to get him into the Hampton Institute in Virginia so he could learn carpentry," Warren says. "It was primarily a trade school and had various kinds of self-help programs, where you could work and go to school.

"But Professor Lee needed Ed's signature. It wouldn't have cost him anything, but Ed wouldn't sign it. Ed didn't see that going to school was of any benefit to young African-American kids, because all they were going to do was work in menial jobs."

Warren saw something recently that sort of captured Ed's attitude.

"There was a cartoon in the paper that had a youngster that had just finished college, lying on the couch still in his cap and gown, and the mother says to him, 'get off the couch, take off that cap and gown, and put on your McDonald's uniform.'

"When we grew up, my dad, his vision was that the only thing you're ever going to do is work on the farm some place, so why go to college? That was the rationale."

Clifton never became a carpenter. He scraped by on Oklahoma Hill. He worked in the box factory. He was poor, but for the most part, his family grew up and did just fine. He had four sons, and three of his daughters-in-law, Agnes, Frances, and her sister Vivian all live in Sykesville today and attend church with Warren on Sundays.

Clifton's daughter Eliza made it through college and taught 30 years of elementary school. His youngest daughter, Grayson, married a man named Richard Dixon, who she met in high school. Dixon would later become the first black treasurer of the state of Maryland and twice win election as a state delegate from Carroll County, a rare feat for a black man and a Democrat in a county where Democrats are outnumbered two to one and blacks make up some five percent of the population.

Thirty-five years after Ed didn't sign that paper, Clifton fell into a mysterious coma. And unlike Chester, when Clifton heard the wings of angels flapping, he did not come back to tell about it. They buried him behind St. Luke's church, where his daughters Hazel and Thelma still come to service once a week.

In 1961, it was Rom's turn. He'd started out under his father at Springfield as an apprentice cook, but Ed was a tough boss and Rom quit. He moved up the road to Henryton and lived in staff housing till he married Gladys, who worked there as a nurse.

He once churned up a field of potatoes with his car, poured cooking grease into his crankcase, raised chickens and sold eggs, lost a hand in an apple shredder, and managed many years with a stub, a joke, and a smile.

But he was a heavy smoker and died from throat cancer at the age of 48. They buried him in the family plot between the four Ds, just a few feet from his mom and dad. Only, Rom got there before they did, and he's the only one of their children buried there today.

Catherine

By 1961, with two brothers buried, there were still three of the original 14 at the house, Ed, Carrie, and Catherine. All the Dorseys were different, but Catherine was different in different ways. She was born in 1925 with two very crooked legs, and for years she walked on metal braces that never quite bent her legs back into shape. She was also prone to seizures and the fairly common malady of not wanting to go to school.

Warren says, "Catherine had educational challenges. At the time they weren't recognized as something that could be addressed, and even if my mother had known how to address them, I don't know that there would have been any resources to do it.

"When it came time for her to go to school she didn't want to go, and the only way my mother could get her to go was having Rosie, who wasn't old enough to start yet, go with her."

So Rosie started early. She was a year and a half younger than Catherine, and every day, they walked to the schoolhouse together.

"Rosie was a very bright young lady," Warren says. "She picked up on what was going on in the classes. They were always together up through high school, and Catherine to some extent was dependent upon Rosie."

Rosie excelled. Catherine struggled. Eventually Rosie finished high school ahead of her sister and went away to college at 15. But she never abandoned Catherine.

"Rosie always helped her," Warren says. "Throughout her adult life, Rosie and Mae were Catherine's major benefactors. And the various nursing places where she was housed, Rosie and Mae saw to it that she was provided for and even up until Catherine died, they always visited her."

Although Catherine was not smart in the conventional sense, or not suited to traditional methods of learning, she could read, and she also had some unusual abilities.

Warren says, "Catherine had a tremendous memory. She knew dates. She knew birds. She knew the tag numbers of every car that came up the road. She knew who owned the car. She knew the makes. She remembered everything about cars.

"Just out of thin air, she would know in detail about a lot of stuff it's surprising anybody would know. With certain kinds of information, she could give complete details, but in other areas she seemed completely blank. And she never cared too much about regular schoolwork.

"By today's standards, she might have been classified as autistic. But the kind of services that might have identified it weren't available. She made it through high school, but she didn't perform very well, and they had no special programs for her. So Catherine suffered."

Down the hill in Sykesville, just over the river—a 15-minute walk from the home on the farm—were the two bars and an area behind them called the beach.

Warren says, "Catherine felt out of place with her own siblings, so she found acceptance with a group that was outside the family and was not socially acceptable to the family. A lot of people used to hang around down at the saloon, down on the beach, which means they couldn't go inside, and they congregated in back outside down near the water, and that's where Catherine spent much of her time when she was in her twenties."

The family didn't like it, but there wasn't much they could do about it.

"If you tried to rationalize with Catherine, she argued," Warren says. "She didn't want us telling her how she should live, and it became a kind of emotional relationship that caused my mother a lot of distress."

For a time, Catherine worked cleaning houses where white people lived. But she never ventured far from home, never developed enough independence to leave the old farm, and never did till near the end.

"The tragedy with Catherine is, my mother didn't understand what her needs were, and some of us, early on, were not as benevolent toward Catherine as we should have been. I've often had regrets about that. But Rosie always stood by her.

"If we had understood Catherine, her life might have been much different, and I've often felt, in retrospect, that we let Catherine down."

Carrie Leaves the Farm

Carrie turned 70 in 1956. She spent most of her time cooking, taking care of the house, and watching after Catherine and Ed. She was older now, heavyset and gray, uncomplicated, dedicated, and nice. She was most comfortable taking care of others.

When quiet Rob Dorsey came to visit, she made sure he had some homemade root beer and cookies. Susan remembers the cookies in tins, and a candy dish full of Mary Janes, and how on Christmas and her birthday, she got a card from Carrie with 10 dimes taped inside.

Carrie had a favorite saying. "You can believe them cherries." It meant something like, "You got that right."

Early in 1963, Carrie was diagnosed with colon cancer. There wasn't a lot they could do in those days, and anyway, they caught it too late. Soon she was very ill. She stayed at the farm till she couldn't anymore. She moved into a nursing place in Baltimore, and just nine months from the diagnosis, on October 10, 1963, the heart that drove the Dorsey machine beat one last time, then stopped.

Warren was 42. Carrie would have been 78 on her birthday. The funeral was at the Haight Funeral Home a couple miles from Oklahoma Hill on Route 32 heading up to Eldersburg. A long procession of cars followed the hearse to Bushy Park Cemetery on the land where Carrie and Ed first met as barefoot kids among grownups who used to belong to white people.

They dug the hole a few feet from the stone with Romulus Dorsey's name on it and not that far from another stone that said Catherine and John Dorsey. And with a big crowd of Dorseys crowding the land where it all began, they lowered Carrie into the earth inside that rectangle of grass defined by four concrete blocks with chiseled Ds.

After the funeral, Ed went back to his room. He didn't seem noticeably changed. There were just two now, Ed and Catherine, sharing the old house and having very little to do with one another. It would stay that way for years to come.

OLD RADIOS

In 1967, Glenn Dorsey decided to pursue a degree in electrical engineering at Drexel University in Philadelphia. On the way there in Warren's car, he got very sick. They spent a lot of time at the Maryland House rest stop on I-95 then continued on to Philadelphia, where for the most part, Glenn hated it.

He grew a beard. He grew an Afro. The campus was at 33rd and Market, just west of the Schuylkill River. The freshman dorm was a ten-story high-rise that Glenn compared to a jail.

He says, "South of school was the University of Pennsylvania, which is a big campus. East was more of the business district. So south and east were not too terribly bad, but north and west you were getting into gang territory.

"There were a lot of gang members returning from Vietnam, who'd learned how to kill people very nicely. So they kind of used what they learned in Nam on the streets of Philadelphia. There were places you really didn't want to go, right off campus. I don't think I ever ventured two blocks north of the dorm."

After freshman year, Glenn moved across the river to New Jersey and commuted to Drexel. The population of Philadelphia in 1968 was just less than two million and closely split between black and white, but at Drexel, the black students all knew one another and calculated they represented one tenth of one percent of the student body.

In New Jersey, Glenn was free now from the prison of the dorms. He missed home, but his biggest problem had nothing to do with the city or living conditions or whether or not he had friends.

He says, "Keep in mind that Frederick High School in 1967, when I graduated, was very good at training farmers and not much else. The agricultural program at Frederick High was probably their shining star. College prep was woefully deficient. So I hit Drexel and met students from places like Baltimore Polytechnic and City College and a lot of the private schools, and I was woefully unprepared.

"I realized on the first day that I was having to run full speed to keep up, and I couldn't keep up. I took high school physics, or what they called physics at Frederick. My first day at Drexel, when I took my first physics class, I decided what I had in high school was not physics. I don't know what it was, but it was not physics.

"So it showed on my transcript that I had a year of physics and made good grades, and they were assuming since I had a year, it would start out as review, but it was all new from day one. I started out behind and got more behind.

"I struggled for three years. I saw the handwriting on the wall with Laplace transforms. I never could master Laplace transforms. The fact that I hated the school didn't help any, but if I could have gotten through Laplace transforms I probably would have stuck it out."

He quit. He was disappointed, but mainly relieved. Warren was disappointed, too, and not relieved.

"In the second half of his junior year, he said he was coming home," Warren says. "And for a week or more, he just sat at home. And I told him, 'You were at a school, your fees were paid, you had an opportunity to get an education, and you chose to leave it without our knowing, but you are not going to sit here and do nothing. You're going to find a job and pay your share of the expenses. We'll keep a record and return every penny if you go back to school.'"

On the SATs, Glenn scored among the top minority kids in the country, but it didn't work out at Drexel. So he came home, sat around, Warren gave him the speech, and eventually Glenn went to Hood College in Frederick while working nights, did quite well, and graduated with a dual major in math and Departmental Honors in economics.

While going to school he worked full time in electronics, and after graduating Hood, he joined NASA at the Goddard Space Center, where they launched satellites, and Glenn worked on launches, "tracking those suckers," as he puts it.

It was great fun, but when NASA began contracting things out, and he did less work and more watching contractors do work, he followed family tradition and headed on to Fort Detrick, where for 25 years he worked with computers, mostly mainframes, doing just about everything, programming in Cobol, data analysis, system administration, and his specialty, database administration.

Glenn says, "Any dummy can build a database. They have books at Barnes and Noble that say databases for dummies. Extracting the data from the database, that takes somebody that knows how the database is put together. And I was quite good at getting the information out of databases."

Today Glenn has nothing to do with Laplace transforms, tracking satellites, or deftly coaxing data from databases. He has big mutton-chop sideburns that stop maybe an inch of chin space short of a beard. He's missing a top front tooth. He's graying and in his mid-sixties and lives in a home in the woods that he heats with wood and shares with a cat.

Warren calls him "a picker" and "a hoarder."

He says, "If Glenn saw a bottle cap, he would get it, old, dirty, rusty bottle caps. He had bags of them. He goes to auctions and yard sales. He's got some of everything. He collects books and sells them at a place in Frederick called Wonder Books that buys them by the pound. I have a small truck he uses to go to sales, and he has so much stuff stashed in his place that he leaves the stuff he takes to the sales in the truck. My truck is one of his storage places."

Glenn got married for a bit, but that didn't work out. He retired from Detrick after 25 years. He bought two and a half acres in the woods, spent a couple years clearing a building space on his own with a chain saw and an axe, had someone build him a house, and eventually moved into his house in the woods and dedicated himself more than anything to collecting old records and old radios.

He has about 8000 records, mostly 33s, mostly classical. He specializes in medieval and renaissance music, music that goes back to the year 1100 or so, and surprisingly, a lot of people record it. That might sound like a lot of records, but Glenn's not impressed.

"A good friend who's a collector and a dealer has somewhere around 400,000 at last count. He has a warehouse. When you say large record collection to my friend, Steve, a large collection is 10,000 and up. I'm probably in the medium range."

Mainly he collects records so he can listen to them. He's not a stereo fanatic or what you might call an audiophile. He has a pair of large Klipsch speakers from the sixties that weigh about 150 pounds apiece. He has transistor amplifiers and tube amplifiers and a mostly modest stereo system.

He knows the music well. At Hood, along with the mathematics and the economics, he also studied music, and in most cases all the other students in his music classes were music majors. In his house in the woods, WBJC Baltimore plays non-stop classical music.

He also has lots of books but doesn't consider himself a collector, or even much of a reader.

"I'm not sure I collect books, but I do have a great number. I accumulate them. Now that I'm retired I have a lot more time for reading, and since my body's started to fall apart it's easier to sit in a chair and read, as long as my eyes hold up, than go out and play in the woods."

But he would prefer playing in the woods.

"There's always something to do in the woods. Since I heat with wood 100 percent, there's always trees to fell and split and cut."

The house is about 3000 square feet, and when I ask how much is taken up with books, records, and radios, without hesitating, he says, "Most of it."

He's got maybe 100 radios now. He has his own stock of vacuum tubes. He has his own test equipment, oscilloscopes, signal generators, multimeters, spectrum analyzers, and things of that nature.

His goal is to get the radios looking good and working. Once they're working, he's not really interested in listening to them. They're all AM and there's nothing on AM he wants to hear.

"We have an antique radio club," he says. "There's 700 or 800 members. Other people communicate through the Internet. I don't believe in the Internet. I worked in that field way too long. I turned the two computers off in my office the day I retired and decided I'd see how long it would be before I turned another computer on. So far it's been almost 11 years."

The radios are mostly for display, but he would prefer to get them working if possible.

"I try to specialize in about 1926 and prior. The first broadcasts were around 1921. The government was doing a lot before that, and there were experimenters playing around, but the first broadcast was '21, so that's basically when the first home entertainment radios were produced."

Warren says, "Glenn comes here Sunday nights and Wednesday nights. He does his laundry sometimes. His real mission, I know, is keeping a check on his parents. He doesn't like when I climb up on the roof, for whatever reason. But he doesn't criticize me. And he doesn't make suggestions unless he's asked. He's not judgmental."

And when he's not in the woods cutting trees or out searching for music first played before Columbus arrived in America, he spends his time collecting more things, chopping at trees in the woods, and breathing life into radios designed when Warren was learning to walk and built before Warren stepped inside the schoolhouse on Oklahoma Hill and began his education.

They are the radios of his father's youth, most from a time when Oklahoma Hill had no electricity and Asa Hepner ran his music emporium on Main Street.

BLUE COLLARS AND JAZZ

From the beginning, Rob was usually the smartest kid in class. He may have been bored, but he made friends and did fine. He went to an all-black school first and second grade, but mixed schools after that.

He attended West Frederick Junior High and then Frederick High. He played JV basketball and ran track and says he was determined, but not really very good at either. He played piano from a very young age, and one day someone brought a Dave Brubeck album home, and Rob discovered his passion in life, which is jazz music.

At some point in his teens, he started to change. He became very quiet, silent almost, withdrawn and distant from his parents, who were left with their suspicions and speculations, but no real understanding.

Warren says, "Rob was a very bright kid. He had a superior IQ. In fact, he belongs to Mensa. And I think that rather than be rewarded by his own community for his intelligence, the tendency was to penalize these people, to ostracize them. And I think he might have been subjected to what we might call bullying.

"He has never mentioned what specifically happened, but he became more and more withdrawn, especially during the latter part of his high school days."

Rob's explanation is simple. He was never bullied or punished for being a smart black kid. There was no specific incident that motivated his mysterious behavior. It's just that things changed around him in ways he didn't like.

He says, "In high school it really seemed the people from my class, the academic class, they changed. Whites and blacks used to more or less hang out together, and it didn't seem to cut across racial lines, but in high school, whites started hanging out with whites and blacks started hanging out with blacks.

"There were other blacks there, but they were mostly from the projects and whatnot. They weren't in the academic curriculum. There were quite a few. Frederick High School had about 900 students, and it was, I would say, somewhere between 15 and 20 percent black, and I didn't feel like I fit in with either group. The whites wanted to hang out with whites and I wasn't white, and the blacks were mostly, like I say, from the projects, and I didn't fit in with them.

"And my parents were also very strict. So a lot of the things that other kids were doing, I basically wasn't allowed to do, so I felt like I didn't fit in anywhere. That's the reason I wanted to go to a black college. That's why I went to

Howard. To find people that were like me, looking to get an education and get ahead."

It added up to a sort of loneliness, resentment, confusion. He was 16, 17, and sort of alone, unable to make friends, frustrated somewhat with his parents, and so he withdrew. He didn't explain. He just did it.

The summer after high school he took a job in Frederick at a factory where they made pots and pans. He worked on the assembly line with a white guy named Floyd. It was grueling.

"You're just pulling pots and pans and other sorts of kitchen type objects off and on this assembly line all day. It was piecework. You got paid a certain base wage and depending on the number of pieces you produced, you got extra. So there was pressure to keep up with the machine, because that could affect not only your wages, but also the guy you were working with.

"If I was slowing down the machine, then I was taking money out of his pocket, too. My hands used to be very sore. And on the assembly line they had these racks, and you could get hit in the head with one of these racks, so you were required to wear a helmet.

"And sometimes you had to work on Saturday mornings. They had these vats of fluid they used to nickel plate the different pots and pans. So you'd climb up on top of these vats and the tops were very slippery. There was maybe a one-inch edge. It might have been larger. But if you slipped, you would fall in the vat. And the vat was acid, basically. And you could see steam coming off the fluid. I never knew of anyone that fell in, but it was dangerous."

When that summer ended, he enrolled full-time in Frederick Community College and took a job at the I-70 truck stop two nights a week.

"And the truck stop job was kind of dangerous, too, because you had these huge trucks coming in all the time to get gas and service, and sometimes you wouldn't see them. It's like you're going between trucks to service a truck and here comes another truck just roaring in, and they're on you before you see them.

"It was a dirty, filthy job, filling them with gas and putting the oil in, putting transmission fluid in, cleaning the windows. My job was the graveyard shift, like twelve to eight, and this was in the middle of winter and it was freezing cold.

"But it was the type of job I really wanted, because this was a side of life I hadn't experienced. I wanted those types of blue-collar jobs, because I felt I'd been sheltered, and I wanted to experience what other people were like in a different side of life.

"This is what people went through. At the assembly line job, the guy I worked with had been there 20 years. My God, how can people do that for 20 years? That's awful. Here I am, I'm young, and my hands are just sore as heck. I'm not going to do this all my years."

The next year was 1973, and he transferred to Howard University as a sophomore, and to Warren's eyes, despite Rob's year of community college and his blue-collar experience at pan factories and truck stops, his outward behavior hadn't changed. They'd had the annual family reunion on Labor Day and Rob had seemed as quiet and withdrawn as ever.

Warren says, "I took him to Howard. We entered the dormitory, and his roommate had a group of friends in the room and a lot of loud music going, and I knew Rob didn't like it. We got the bags out of the trunk, and Rob just took them and walked away without a word. He never looked back. That was probably the hardest moment of my life.

"On one or two occasions I brought him home for visits. From the time I picked him up on campus till the time we got home, he didn't say one word."

Rob doesn't remember the loud music and the roommate, and anyway, by his next semester he had a room of his own. He was unaware of his father's feelings about their departure. He was just happy for his independence and hopeful he would fit in better in college than high school. He studied anthropology.

"I was interested in human nature. Anthropology is the study of man. In particular it's the study of other cultures."

He still kept mainly to himself. He did well in school, but after sophomore year, he took a year off to try to figure out what to do with his life. Plus he wanted to save up for a car.

That summer he worked on the highway as a construction helper, and in September, he moved on to another fairly dangerous job, this time in a metal shop producing construction beams. He painted beams, punched holes in them, worked a saw, cut beams with a torch, ground the rough edges off, tried his hand at welding and discovered it was an art he would never master.

He says, "It was inside, but they had these big doors at each end and they'd move the metal in one end and the finished pieces out the other. So it'd get real cold in the winter. While they had the doors closed it would warm up some, but they wouldn't keep the doors closed long, because they were constantly moving metal in and out and you'd get frozen, and that happened all day.

"And I used to come home filthy, because they were welding and grinding all these metal beams, and when I blew my nose, it was black from breathing in all that metal dust."

Freezing in a metal shop and sneezing up particles of black metal wasn't his initial plan for the year off.

"I wanted to get a job down in the South and live in the South to have that experience. And I picked Hattiesburg, Mississippi. I don't know how I came up with Hattiesburg. And my father didn't want me to go at all. I'd heard so much about the South and discrimination and the problems there, and I wanted to experience that for myself, but they didn't let me go."

Warren says, "Rob always had empathy for people who were less fortunate, and at one point, he told me he wanted to room in the inner city. He wanted to experience the life of the ghetto in Washington, the life of the poor people.

"I didn't permit it. I told him, anytime you want to know about the life of a poor person, if you have a couple of days, I'll tell you all about it."

Rob doesn't seem to remember wanting to live in the ghetto, and Warren doesn't seem to remember the thing about Mississippi, but they both agree on one thing, Rob got his car, a Ford Pinto he picked up for $3000.

When he returned to Howard junior year, he rented a room in the home of a nice old black woman who lived by herself. Her name was Gustava Brown and they became friends. He lived with her his last two years of college. When he graduated, Gustava was there.

He finished with honors in anthropology. IBM hired him as a computer analyst in their research facility in San Jose, California.

"He took off in his little Pinto to California," Warren remembers. "When he left, he waved goodbye and said, 'I'm off to California.' He worked at IBM in San Jose for two years."

Eventually, he returned east and worked as a computer analyst, got tired of that, applied to 15 law schools and got accepted at 14. While still in his twenties he attended the University of Texas Law School, then switched to the University of Maryland and received an MBA and a law degree.

He took a job with a law firm in Baltimore. After that, he came to Frederick County and worked in the State's Attorney's Office as Assistant State's Attorney for about a year and a half, working mostly juvenile cases.

He was a Democrat. When power shifted to the Republicans he moved on and took a job with a software company. Eventually he quit that and recently took another master's degree, this one in information management from the University of Maryland.

Probably if he had his way, Rob wouldn't work in computers or law. He'd be a jazz piano player. Well, he is a jazz piano player, just not the kind who gets paid money and makes a living at it. But that's what gets him excited.

Warren says, "Rob never performs for anybody. Except, one night about a year ago, he wanted to know if I wanted to go to a concert. And I said, 'Rob, really I'm not up to going to any concert.' We were in the basement and he said, 'all you have to do is go upstairs and I'll do a concert for you.' So we did. He had a list of about 600 songs that he does from memory. And he played for about two hours."

Rob's not convinced his father likes his music. He recently put a collection of his songs on his father's computer, showed him how to play them, and wrote up instructions. A few months later, he asked Warren if he ever played the songs.

"I said, 'Dad, did you listen to the songs I gave you last year?' My father says, 'Oh yeah, yeah, I listen to them every now and then. I just pull the tape recorder out and I listen to them.' I said, 'Tape recorder? I didn't put them on a tape recorder. You can't be listening to them on a tape recorder.'"

Baby, Too, Can Fly

Glenn is 11 years older than Susan. Rob is six. Her brothers were academically brilliant and musically gifted. Her mother was a first-grade teacher. Her father was a scientist. They were an intellectual family who discussed algebra at the dinner table. She spent her early days among older family, feeling young and unnoticed.

"And so I spent my whole life trying to be relevant," Susan says. "My dad, even though he doesn't like to admit this, he sort of left me out of stuff because I was a girl. They would go fishing and leave me home, and his famous saying was, 'Baby wait a little longer, until baby's wings are a little stronger, and baby too can fly.'

"I think that probably shaped my being. I was determined I was going to do anything anybody else could do and never be left out."

She attended a special kindergarten on Fort Detrick with mostly military kids. She was one of two blacks. She moved on to South Frederick Elementary School. The school was experimenting with a program called Open Space. It was six years and self-paced. Susan finished all the work in five and spent the sixth grade bored, ignored, and frustrated.

She attended the same junior high as her brothers, but by the time she started in 1972, Glenn and Rob were both long gone. For the most part, Susan had only one thing in common with them anyway. She was a natural musician, and their musical reputation preceded her.

She says, "Everybody made a big deal about Rob having perfect pitch, and again, I'm trying to be relevant, so let's say he's ten, and they're all marveling that they hit a note on the piano, and he tells them the note, and I would go, 'Well I can do that.' And I could. I had perfect pitch too.

"So the minute I walked into seventh grade band, the instructor didn't say anything, he just looked at me. He knew who I was. He hit a note on the piano, and waited for me to tell him what it was, and of course I did, and he goes, 'Yep, you've got it, too.'"

While the sixties exploded around her, Susan barely noticed. She was four and still riding her dad's back to bed each night when John Kennedy died. She was eight the year Martin Luther King, Jr., died and then Robert Kennedy. The Vietnam War was background noise. She lived a safe, sheltered, middle-class life with two smart, talented, hard-working, and very strict parents. She spent most of her early years performing in one way or another.

She says, "I was always on stage. I did my first piano recital at four. In high school they found out I could sing, which, well when you grow up with my parents, in comparison, I really couldn't sing.

"I danced. I performed in plays and musicals. I was a pretty renowned flutist. I was in honor band. I was in All-County. I was first chair. I was in the Mid-east All-Star band, and went to Pittsburgh to play in that my senior year. So that was kind of my thing."

At one point she joined a jazz band that didn't need a flute, so she taught herself sax. She took Rob's clarinet and learned that, too.

"Music was a constant in our house. Both my parents were in the church choir. My mother directed the youth choir. She taught piano to the neighborhood children in our house.

"Both my parents could have been professional singers, but they opted to raise three children instead. The three of us learned piano early and then musical instruments beginning in 4th grade. We were all selected to play at our high school graduations, Glenn and I as soloists, and Rob as the accompanist to the soloist."

Some of her friends were black; some were white. She liked everyone, and everyone liked her. If something needed doing, she did it. When they needed a traffic light for a dance, she got them a traffic light.

"I think I was the dance committee chairman, and for one of the dances, the theme was 'The Long and Winding

Road,' so my vision was a traffic light and this long kind of road going up onto the stage in the gym.

"And I called the city and said, 'Hey do you have any traffic lights?' I guess I'm sort of fearless, but in my mind, it was like, why wouldn't they have a traffic light? And they did."

Warren helped her pick up the light, load it on the truck, and take it to the gym.

When she was 15, she went to Russia. It was 1975. Nixon had resigned. Gerald Ford was president. It was late in the era of détente, when Nixon and Brezhnev initiated a thaw in American-Soviet relations. She was a delegate from the National Council of American-Soviet Friendship and spent the summer in the Soviet Union at the All-Union Young Pioneer Camp on the Crimean Peninsula near Yalta where once, in February 1945, Stalin, Churchill, and a very sick and soon to be dead FDR met to hash out the details of a new post-war order.

The camp held 5000 kids from 62 countries, including 12 Americans. She spent 10 days in Moscow. She took trips to Kiev and Sevastopol. There were musical competitions and cultural excursions. She won a bronze medal in swimming.

One of the Soviet counselors was in the Communist party, but for Susan it had very little to do with politics.

"At 15, I just mostly liked being away from home and experiencing all kinds of new things—taking a hydrofoil down the Moscow River, going to the Moscow Circus, eating Russian ice cream, seeing Red Square and Lenin's tomb, including Lenin's body. He'd been dead 50 years."

Her senior year she was elected president of the student council.

"I think the school was 20 percent African American, but I hung out with everybody. I guess that's why I sort of won in a landslide, because while I was in class with what might be the intelligent clique, I got along with everybody."

She graduated from Frederick High School in 1978 and chose her college on her own, mainly because by then she and her dad were having a bit of a war.

"He will not tell you he was terribly overprotective, but he was terribly overprotective," she says. "We had different rules than the other kids. It was sort of embarrassing. Like if parties were over at midnight, I had to leave at 11. They would be house parties, and people would go, 'Oh, Susan, your father's at the door.'

"He'd pick me up at 11 for a party that was over at 12. I knew that was the deal, and I just kind of lived with that. I was like, 'whatever,' I'm just going to go through all the hoops, because I'm going to the party. I might have to leave early, but I wasn't going to be left out of anything.

"There were a lot of things like that. Kids would get on the city bus and go to the mall, and we weren't allowed to do that."

And she's right, Warren won't tell you he was terribly overprotective, or even that he was extra strict. What he'll tell you is this.

"Susan has always wanted to command her life. In this household, this didn't always work as smoothly as desired. I told the kids, Rob and Glenn in particular, I don't remember what the issue was, Glenn is about six-five, and he's very hefty, and I told him, as long as he lived under my roof, that I am the tallest and biggest man in this house."

Which, mathematically speaking, wasn't quite true. Warren is five feet and seven inches tall, which would make him about 10 inches shorter than his oldest son.

On the question of his strictness, he says, "That was their perception. I am an extension of my mother in many ways. She was a loving woman, but my mother had an unwritten code of behavior, and you had to abide by it. And there were consequences if you strayed. Carrie was an easygoing person, as long as you stayed within the rules of that house.

"I wanted them to do well. They knew there were certain things required. You're going to behave at school, and you're going to behave in any place when you're away from this house.

"You're going to do things on time, you're going to go to school on time, and you go every day. You're going to do your best to learn as much as you can from every experience. I expected them to do well at school. And the first indication of trouble, we'd be at school.

"I remember distinctly the center of black life in Frederick was on one street we used to live on. They opened a youth center, and I didn't consider it well-managed, and Glenn was the older kid, and he mentioned this center, and

I told him forget it, you're not going, don't even bring this subject up, because you're not going.

"I guess I came across pretty strict. The kids even told me they were afraid of me. I said, 'How can anyone be afraid of me?' Nobody could have loved their kids more than we loved ours. But we were demanding of them, yes."

Whether Warren was adhering to a set of rules, being reasonable in his way, or not, Susan hated it. She says, "My father and I were always at loggerheads, and my mother would come along to referee. My last year of high school, I could not wait to get out of the house."

Warren suggested community college. Susan suggested she'd rather sling hamburgers at McDonald's.

"I wanted to major in architecture," she says, "I've always been fascinated by buildings and structures and kind of constructing things. I remember building furniture for my dolls as a ten- or twelve-year-old. And maybe an influence is that my dad was always Mr. Fix-it, and I was his helper.

"And I was kind of a math whiz, which is funny to think about now. So with the creative and the math ability, it sort of made sense to be an architect. It had to be a school of architecture and of the highest academic standing, and that's how I made the decision.

"And my father didn't really participate, because as far as I was concerned, he wasn't being reasonable. Like if he was actually going to have me at community college, I thought that was ridiculous. So I did all the research and applied for early admission."

She chose the University of Virginia, the school founded by Thomas Jefferson in 1819. She started in 1978. She got her degree in architecture in 1982. She moved to Richmond and worked for State Farm as an insurance adjustor, moved into technology integration, then got interested in marketing and returned to the University of Virginia, and by 1987, she had her MBA from the Darden School of Business.

She took a job with IBM in Richmond and worked there in a number of sales and marketing positions for 19 years. Not long after moving to Richmond, she got involved at her alma mater by signing up as an interviewer for the school's Jefferson Scholars program. She started out interviewing applicants, moved up to team captain, and eventually became chair of the entire process.

She was also on the board of a non-profit learning center dedicated to helping kids in public housing in Richmond develop computer skills. There were centers in various housing communities to provide afterschool programming.

She says, "Computers weren't ubiquitous like now, and clearly they didn't have them in the house, and this was an opportunity for the have-nots to have a bit of an advantage in computer literacy. Each learning center was like a community building for the public housing with its own offices and a computer lab."

United States Senator Tim Kaine, who was then a Richmond City Councilman, and who went on to become

Governor of Virginia, was also on the board, and they became friends.

In 1996, another future governor and senator, Mark Warner, was preparing a senate run, and decided to visit one of these learning centers. Susan escorted him, and they, too, became friends.

Warner was on the board of Virginia Union University in Richmond, one of the state's five historically black colleges.

Susan says, "And this was sort of the lead-up to Y2K, where none of the companies could find people to hire, because the world was coming to an end, and Mark wondered why tech brands didn't recruit at Virginia Union. Historically, it had been a liberal arts college, and the high-tech firms didn't realize that all five historically black colleges in Virginia had management and information systems, computer science, and systems engineering degrees."

Warner founded an organization called the Virginia High-Tech Partnership to try to connect the high-tech companies with these black colleges.

When he won the governorship in 2001, Warner was forced to put all his money into a blind trust. Since he could no longer run it, he established a board of directors to run the Virginia High-Tech Partnership and appointed Susan to the board. Eventually she became chair of that organization, too.

By 2002, Warner was governor of Virginia. He ran into Susan at a Christmas party and asked her to arrange a meeting through "his people." In February 2003, she met with Warner in the governor's office.

He said, "Do you know why you're here?"

She said, "I have no idea."

He appointed her to the University of Virginia's Board of Visitors, a group of 16 voting members (there are 17 now), who oversee the operation of the school. The president of the university reports to them.

When Tim Kaine was elected governor in 2005, he reappointed Susan to another four-year term, during which John T. Casteen III, the university's president of 20 years, retired. The school created a special committee to replace him. There were 19 members, including Susan, who examined more than 190 applications. When the board settled on Teresa Sullivan, it was Susan who put Sullivan's name up for nomination.

She has a knack for taking over organizations and acquiring influence without actually setting out to do so. She also has a knack for meeting very famous politicians mostly by accident. One day while attending a convention in D.C., she was heading to her car in the parking deck, when she ran into Barack Obama.

He was a state legislator from Illinois. He'd just spoken at the convention. She was heading to her car. He was heading to his. He introduced himself to Susan, and she wished him luck in his campaign for senate.

Mostly what she remembers of the encounter was the future president's physique.

"He was skinny, skinnier even than he looks."

She lives in a nice home in Richmond that, by another coincidence, used to belong to Paul Cantor, one of three Cantor brothers. They ran a construction development company in Virginia. Susan lives in Virginia's 7th Congressional district, and Paul Cantor's brother was Susan's congressman, Republican Eric Cantor, another famous skinny guy, number two in the House leadership, and one of the skinny President's archenemies, until Cantor's totally unexpected defeat to an unknown Tea Party candidate in the 2014 Republican primary.

"We're friends," she says. "In fact my house was built before Eric ran for congress. He was still a state delegate at the time. Paul built the house for himself, and I bought it from Paul, and I used to have these big Christmas brunches, and my friend Jackie is a dear friend of Diana Cantor, Eric's wife, and she said Diana wanted to come to the brunch to see what the house looked like since Paul moved out, and that's how I met Diana.

"She's a dear. Their kids are great. They're great people. We just disagree on politics."

She attended Obama's first Inaugural with tickets provided by Eric Cantor. Before the Inauguration, she attended breakfast in his office with a small group of others.

You can only serve two terms on the Board of Visitors, but through her work on the university's alumni association and various foundations and scholarship committees, her work with the university continues.

She says, "I have a lot of kids, a lot of nieces and nephews and people who call me mom or whatever that I've met over time from UVA through these scholarship programs. They send me pictures of their babies, and all kinds of stuff."

In a speech at the University of Virginia's Black Women's Leadership Dinner in 2008, speaking of her position on the Board of Visitors she said, "With this unintended power comes a great responsibility."

She said, "I have spent a great deal of time interacting with kids beginning with...those Jefferson Scholars interviews...I feel a great deal of pride in carrying the torch for all who believe no one has played that role before. And I challenge myself to consider the needs of the underrepresented in all of the decisions I'm asked to make."

Not long before giving that speech, in November 1, 2007, Susan had a complete mastectomy of the right breast. Her parents came down on October 31 and took her in for surgery.

She'd never really been in the hospital before. She didn't like the idea of spending the night after the operation in a hospital bed alone, so she brought along a stuffed polar bear named Polaris that an old boyfriend gave her back in the eighties.

"Polaris normally wears a yellow ribbon around his neck," she says. "But I took off his yellow ribbon and put on a pink ribbon for the occasion."

The surgery was scheduled for 8, but got delayed till closer to noon. The waiting room was packed.

She says, "So my parents are sitting in the waiting room all this time. When I finally got in my room after surgery, it was late afternoon, and my father comes in with my bag and my bear. And I said, 'What did you do with the bear?' And he said, 'Oh I had him with me.'

"I said, 'You held the bear all this time?' And Poppi's pretty manly, and he's like, 'Well yeah.'"

Susan asked him what the other people in the waiting room said.

Warren said, "I don't know those people. You wanted the bear, and I don't know those people."

Carolyn was 85. Warren was 87. Polaris was in his early twenties. Together, the three of them waited for hours in the crowded waiting room, Carolyn, Warren, and a giant white bear with a pink bow around his neck.

Susan spent one night in the hospital. She came home on a Friday. Monday she went power walking. Tuesday she sent her parents home.

Susan's grandmother Carrie searched through piles of discarded clothes that Margaret Harris dug up. Carrie's mom was the slave daughter of a slave merchant, and delivered Susan's father in a cold farmhouse without electricity or running water in 1920.

When Carrie died, Susan was three. Carrie could not possibly have imagined that someday the little girl eating cookies and drinking homemade root beer in her kitchen would shake the hand of a president before he quite got there, nominate the president of the university started by Thomas Jefferson, become a global market manager for

IBM, and count as her friends in 2014 both of Virginia's senators and a powerful U.S. congressman.

They call her Syd, short for Susan Y. Dorsey.

Syd calls Senator Mark Warner "Mark," Senator Tim Kaine "Tim," Congressman Eric Cantor "Eric," Warren Dorsey "Poppi," and Barack Obama "skinny." Three are friends, one's her dad, and one is the first black President of the United States.

These are things Carrie could not have dreamed.

Long Live the King

When you look at Glenn, Rob, and Susan, or Warren and Carolyn and the larger extended family, you can't help thinking Ed Dorsey might have been a happy, successful, even great man if he wasn't born the wrong color in the wrong place at the wrong time, if his mother hadn't died young and his father hadn't wandered off.

Ed's sister, Hattie, who was very young when her mother died, moved in with her sister Emma and managed to get both bachelor's and master's degrees from Howard University, get married, and move to Philadelphia and live a long successful life.

Maybe the difference between Hattie and Ed was that someone took her in. Or maybe not. People are shaped by circumstances, but they're also born with talents and tendencies.

Warren says, "The old man had a brilliant mind, but he could not endure the kind of treatment he was accorded in the workplace. He didn't have the personality to rebel physically, and he didn't have the sophistication to change laws.

"The farm was his haven in a sea of discrimination. He thought he could be self-sufficient, and he came close. We only depended marginally on the white community, and he had very little contact with the outside world. He stayed in his room for years and years."

He'd wandered off Bush Park not long after the Civil War and slavery, a teenager with no parents and no money. He'd wandered and learned and brooded and tried to build his sanctuary in Sykesville. He'd held jobs, done them well, and left them.

He had his pool hall in the barn where no one could touch him. He cooked great. He built tools. He shot clay pigeons so well that others would pay him to shoot for them. Which suited Ed fine, because he really liked to shoot, but couldn't afford the entrance fees. He'd shoot, he'd win, and someone else would collect the prize.

He could butcher and preserve a pig, hunt rabbits, cut hair, and fix shoes. He could figure out just about anything, do it quickly, and do it well.

It's possible he was just lazy, but that doesn't seem likely. You can be lazy without staying in your room and avoiding all human contact. There was no TV up there. There was no radio. There was just Ed alone with his thoughts and some things to read.

It's possible he had dark secrets, or as Warren believes, overpowering grievances that sort of crippled him. He wouldn't be the first intelligent black man of his time who found himself sort of powerless and so frustrated that it became almost impossible to move.

In his 1945 memoir *Black Boy*, Richard Wright speaks of his own feelings after losing a promising job in Mississippi due to the malice of two cruel Southern white men.

"For weeks after that I could not believe in my feelings. My personality was numb, reduced to a lumpish, loose, dissolved state. I was a non-man, something that knew vaguely that it was human but felt that it was not. As time separated me from the experience I could feel no hate for the men who had driven me from the job. They did not seem to be individual men, but part of a huge, implacable, elemental design for which hate was futile. What I did feel was a longing to attack. But how? And because I knew of no way to grapple with this thing, I felt doubly cast out.

"I went to bed tired and got up tired, so I was having no physical exercise. During the day I overreacted to each event, my banked emotions spilling around it. I refused to talk to anyone about my affairs, because I knew that I would only hear a justification of the ways of the white folks and I did not want to hear it. I lived carrying a huge wound, tender, festering, and I shrank when I came near anything that I thought would touch it.

"But I had to work because I had to eat."

That could have been Ed. Except rather than an urge to attack, he felt the urge to withdraw, to live with the wound in privacy.

Of course, it's possible he suffered from something more mundane, something that his grievances exacerbated, maybe depression, or some other illness, when there was little understanding of these things and no effective treatment. And besides, if someone had offered him Prozac, Ed would have stuck it on a shelf. He was stubborn, and didn't trust doctors.

"A couple times he got right sick," Warren says. "Once my mother finally convinced him to see a doctor, because he was having chest pains."

The doctor diagnosed a heart problem and gave Ed some pills. Ed brought them home and put them on the kitchen shelf.

Carrie said, "Well, aren't you going to take some of them pills."

And Ed said, "No. My heart's as strong as a bull's."

The doctor died, and Ed lived another 30 years without touching those pills.

On another occasion, a doctor sent him home with a bottle of some sort of amber liquid. Again, Ed put the medicine on the shelf. Again, Carrie said, "Ed, aren't you going to take your medicine?"

Ed said, "No. After he examined me, the doctor went in another room and came out wiping his hands. I think he peed in that bottle."

Rob says, "He was very quiet. He would speak to you, maybe sometimes say a word or two, but he didn't say much. He would just sit in the chair and sort of observe everything going on."

Glenn says, "I remember Granddaddy sitting in front of that stove in the dining room, holding his head in his hands. Every time I went down there, that's where he'd be, sitting in front of the stove, holding his head in his hands, and that's the way he'd be sometimes the entire time we'd visit. At the time I thought that was just him, that was standard procedure.

"After my grandmother died and grandfather was living there by himself, the kids decided he needed a modern cookstove. So they took the old cookstove out and put in a modern stove. It lasted as long as it took him to disconnect the new stove and drag the cookstove back in off the porch and put it back up.

"Within a year or two of when he passed away, he still used that wood fire cookstove, down to the point where he could no longer collect his own wood. So we went down there one fall and cut a bunch of trees off the place and cut them up and stacked them by the house for him."

Susan remembers an older and maybe happier Ed.

"Granddaddy Ed was apparently a vastly changed person in his later years. He loved having his family around and seemed to cherish that time. His children all said he was fairly absent from their lives, even though he lived in the same house, but he was 76 when I was born and passed when I was 19, so I only saw his grandfatherly side.

"I was his youngest grandchild of 43. I remember him being an avid pinochle player, and that we could get him to jump rope when he was in his late eighties."

Warren is forgiving of his father, but he also says this.

"Even though he had kids who needed whatever little money he could bring home for survival, he couldn't take being kicked around, and he would quit. He would just sit in his room. Sometimes we would hardly ever see him.

"Sometimes I tell Susan and Carolyn, I don't know why Carrie didn't kick him out, but she stuck with him."

Warren thinks maybe Ed's problems went all the way back to Africa, that somehow coded in his DNA, Ed Dorsey lived with a sense of superiority that made the prejudice he encountered all the more intolerable.

"We traced Ed's ancestry back to the Central African Republic, and the tribe is the Lissongo. I theorize my daddy came from the ruling class, because he always had this air of importance, a sort of a regal way about him. His sisters did, too, as if they were used to people serving them and could never accept the menial condition imposed on them by segregation."

So maybe that was it. Maybe Ed thought of himself as a king cast unfairly from his kingdom, forced to roam unrecognized and unacknowledged among the common people in some terrible place where no one understood and no one cared, where suddenly he was at the bottom and could see no way back to the top.

Or maybe he just liked being alone. His grandson Glenn lives alone with a cat in a home in the woods with old music and old radios. His other grandson, Rob, spends many a night alone with his piano and his jazz. When Thelma lived with Ed's sister Emma for three years, she rarely saw her aunt. Emma stayed in her room and read one book after another.

Finally, in 1977, after nearly 50 years, Ed abandoned the sanctuary of his farmhouse. He didn't want to leave, but somehow Thelma convinced him. He lived with her awhile, but eventually moved into a nursing home in Baltimore, where he died in 1980 of no specific cause, just an old heart strong as a bull's finally giving out.

They buried him with Carrie and Rom between the four Ds they'd planted in 1942. They buried most of his story with him. We'll never know what went on inside Ed's mind as he sat by the stove with his head in his hands. We'll never know what he did all that time alone in his room. We'll never know how Ed felt when his mother died, and one sister took his brother and one took his youngest sister and he was 14 and no one took him.

We'll never really know where he traveled and what he did and how he survived. We'll never know what happened to him in Baltimore. We'll never know what he regretted, what he dreamed, what he hated, and what he wished he might have been.

The family never celebrated birthdays, except one year when it rained extra and the crops grew and they had extra potatoes, extra everything, a huge harvest, Ed decided to make a giant cake and celebrate all the birthdays at once.

He had a cake decorating kit he'd picked up somewhere and built a cake of many layers covered with delicious icing. But he ran into technical difficulties involving gravity and physics and pans and ingredients, and eventually he realized the only way to build the wonderful cake of many layers he saw in his head was to resort to a more sturdy main ingredient.

So he built the cake of wood and covered it with icing. And maybe that's it. Ed Dorsey was, it seems, a man who never understood the true purpose of a cake. He built a life on a farm. He built a cake out of wood. He just couldn't taste it.

Warren says, "He was 95 when he died. But in all those 95 years, the real Ed Dorsey never emerged. Nobody really knew who he was."

Demolishing the Dream

Standing on Oklahoma Avenue in Sykesville is the old green house where Minnie lives. She's not the last Dorsey in Sykesville, but she's the oldest, and possibly the town's oldest resident. Chester passed away in 2005, but the house they built while Adolph Hitler overran Europe, bombed England, and sent his armies rushing toward Moscow has outlived Hitler's thousand-year Reich by about 70 years now.

Sometime in the forties, with all the boys gone off to work or college or war, the family sold the cows, the pigs, the horses, and shut down the chicken operation. There was no one left to warm the breeder pens, dispense the feed, kill the cockerels, collect and package the eggs. There was no one left to work the ground.

Nature swallowed up the fields, and over the next 30 or 40 years, all signs of the farm slowly grew away. Trees grew and weeds and shrubs and grass. The chicken coops decayed and fell and rotted in the rain and cold and heavy weight of snow. The deer came and the rabbits and squirrels and birds and insects and all the living things that devour and transform an abandoned field and make it their own. Things broke and rusted and fell, and nature swallowed Ed's old dream.

Nobody shot the rabbits anymore. Nobody shot the squirrels and turned them into stew. Nobody hooked up a plow to a genius horse and plowed up potatoes. No one walked into town with a basket of eggs and walked back with sugar or syrup. Old Jack and Old Frank and all the rest of the many animals that ran and hunted and worked and ate on the Dorsey lands were ghosts now and memories.

Susan says, "It wasn't much of a farm by the time I came along. It was pretty overgrown for most of the 40 acres. When I was about 12 or so, Granddaddy hosted an expedition, or 'safari,' we called it, out to what they called 'The Back Place.' I remember about 20 of us on this hike, as Granddaddy recalled what used to be where. He would have been well in his eighties by then."

Catherine lived into her seventies. She was always there when Susan came to visit. She loved to play horseshoes. Eventually Catherine's health began to go. Ed was old and frail, and Rosie and Mae took their sister to a group home, where she stayed for a while before moving to a nursing place, where she died in 2002.

They donated her body to science. The Maryland Anatomy Board gathers bodies and apportions them out to medical schools and colleges for study, before they're cremated and returned.

By coincidence, if the ashes aren't claimed, they're returned to Springfield Hospital in Sykesville, where they're held awhile and then disposed of. And so Catherine's body went off in the name of science, and her ashes came home a year later to the hospital that first brought the Dorseys to Sykesville.

Thelma was already there, waiting. She died on July 22, 2000, and her ashes, too, came home to Springfield.

After Carrie died and Catherine left and finally Ed, the old house sat there. It became rundown and ugly and dangerous. Kids vandalized it. The family made efforts to save it, things got complicated, there were lawyers involved, and eventually it all fell through and the house began to fall. Finally the town of Sykesville ripped the old Dorsey place down and sent the family a bill for $10,000.

Jonathan Herman was mayor. He was a guy who found old buildings and tried his best to save them. But when they tore the old Dorsey place down, he watched the demolition.

Years later, when I told him that was the home where Warren grew up, he was surprised. He'd done more than anyone to revive the town. He'd helped save the schoolhouse, too, but he gives most of the credit for that to Jack

Johnson's son, Eugene Johnson, perhaps the town's only black council member ever.

Herman says, "Gene was instrumental in saving the schoolhouse, and in a very humble and almost indistinguishable way."

But neither Gene Johnson, nor Jonathan Herman, nor anyone else could save the old Dorsey home from the wrecking crew that day. While Herman watched in his baseball cap, as big machines smashed windows, crushed walls, and tore out foundation that clung stubbornly to the earth, the mayor had no idea the old house dying before him was the crumbling remnant of an abandoned dream.

There would be no more sweeping out piles of dead flies, no more Black Flag powder and Pain King, no more chewing up food and feeding it to babies, no more whitewashed walls and beds filled with kids sleeping on hay, no more clothes blowing in the wind or freezing on the line and a young woman and her kids lugging coal up a hill, no more Christmas wreaths in windows and hide and seek in the trees, no more pinochle and peanuts from Baltimore on Christmas mornings, no more sitting silently in the dark during thunderstorms in respect for the Lord.

Where the house once stood, I drove by one day in the cold winter of 2014 and saw an empty lot with a sale sign on it. And beside the sign was a small pile of rubble, some wood, some cinder blocks.

But that's been cleared now. The trash is gone. Just like the pool hall's gone. The farm is gone. The chicken houses and old baseball field are gone. Most of the old houses on Oklahoma Hill are gone.

A couple still stand, and there's the schoolhouse, there's Minnie's place, and a strange little building right beside her house that I'll get to shortly.

And where the Dorsey house once stood, they're digging out and flattening the brown earth one day, then laying the foundation for something new the next. They dig fast, not like the old days, when it took an entire summer to dig the foundation for the home where Minnie lives.

Back then, Warren says, "To dig the foundation, they used a team of horses and a gadget the horses pulled, and we scooped it out with the horses and our hands. It took us most of the summer."

That was more than 80 years ago. Now they use machines. One day there's a pile of trash. A few days later there's a well-organized series of deep connected alleys beneath the earth, like the rat-filled trenches of WWI. And then, almost magically, there's a foundation rising from the ground and painted black, and Minnie's clothes, just yards away, blowing gently on the line in a beautiful August breeze, have something new and strange to stare at.

Something huge is rising from the earth. And soon Minnie will have neighbors with no idea that once, on the ground where their new house stands, for 30,000 days, there had been another house, another family, a great and fascinating drama, and a thousand little tales.

They'll have no idea that the elderly neighbor hanging her clothes on the line behind her house or out watering the flowers on her porch was once a young woman with a letter in her hand and a husband at the brink of death hundreds of miles away. Or that eight decades ago, she went to the prom with a boy named Warren who couldn't dance, but could sing like nothing she'd ever heard.

Faith Calls Warren Home

The church sits up a hill southeast of town and stares through woods down across the busy Route 32. It's a long story how the town saved itself, but the stores on Main Street are full now. Businesses come and go. But they do come. There are two nice restaurants. There are festivals and live music and novelty shops and antiques.

There's a bookstore and a fountain and a small post office built from the reconstructed remains of an old railroad switching station. Across from the post office is a French café with crêpes and gourmet coffee built in a historic building that once stood on Main Street, and then in a parking lot behind Main Street, and was eventually pulled across the lot on a truck and beautifully restored in its current resting place.

Not everyone got it. Not everyone liked it, but the restoration of the town was brilliant, then stalled, and then revived and brilliant again.

It's not a thriving town. It still doesn't have much money, but many of its residents do. And it's alive. It's unique. It's reborn. There's really no place in the world quite like it.

The church where Warren comes is white, and originally the people who went there were white, too. Well, not exactly. You see the church that originally stood on the spot
was called St. Paul's. They dedicated the building in 1878.
But in 1889, St Paul's packed up and moved across the river, disassembling their church, then putting it back together on the other side.

St. Paul's church published a history, and in the history
it tells how "on the last wagon load of stone from the
church, they placed the cornerstone. It had rained and the
road was rutty and full of mud holes. A big engine came
snorting and blowing and whistling down the railroad, and
the off-wheel horse gave a jump, and off went the cornerstone–plop in the mud and water."

They rebuilt their church just off Main Street and left
behind not much more than a hole on two acres of land,
and gave the hole and the land to the black community.
And the black people built a church there and called it St.
Luke's. It's been there ever since, and if you go behind the
church and walk through the small graveyard, you'll dis-
cover that most of the dead are named Dorsey or Norris.

Chester, Everett, and Clifton are all buried there. James
Norris, "the old dude at third," is up there, too.

Warren doesn't like visiting cemeteries. He prefers to
remember people alive and at their best. Sometime in the
nineties, Warren began driving out from Frederick every
Sunday to St. Luke's, not to visit dead relatives or stroll
among the stones and the memories, but to attend services, and mainly to sing. When he was a kid, that church,

along with the house and the old school, was one of the three pillars of his closed-in life.

His mother was very religious, thus the silent gatherings in the living room during thunderstorms, but she did not go to church often. Warren is the opposite, not terribly religious, but fond of attending church.

His thoughts on church and religion and God are complicated now, but when he was a kid, he had no deep thoughts about such things. Church was just part of life.

He remembers Sunday school. He remembers Children's Day on the second Sunday of June, when they'd gather ferns taller than themselves from the hill opposite the schoolhouse, and gather flowers from everyone's yards, and weave them all together and cover the altar and the whole front of the church with ferns and flowers and build an archway of flowers down the aisle that everyone walked through on their way to the pews.

He remembers the old organ that only Gene Norris could play and only by ear and only what he already knew. And he remembers another Dorsey, a man named John who wasn't related to the clan of Carrie and Ed and whose 21-year-old son, Douglas, died instantly with a crushed skull in a car the same week Chester was crushed in a different car. Douglas Dorsey's buried behind the old church, too.

They called Douglas Dorsey's dad "God Almighty John Dorsey," because that was his favorite expression. He couldn't read words, but he could read music and sing the notes and somehow he taught them songs.

And Warren says, "Often when I stand in the church on Sunday mornings and sing, I envision Mr. John Dorsey standing there. One of his favorite expressions was 'sing it out.' His measure of good singing was how loud you sang. And he would say, 'my God Almighty, children, sing it out,' and we would sing it out."

When Warren was a kid, the church had a dirt basement and a potbelly stove for heat. They added a bit to it in the forties and modernized it over time. Warren's the oldest member of a shrinking congregation. Everyone calls him Uncle Tom.

For many years, he attended church and did his singing in Frederick, but near the end of the nineties, as Sykesville resurrected itself, Warren's niece decided to revive the St. Luke's choir.

Her name was Faith Green. She was Clifton's granddaughter, the daughter of Clifton's daughter, Thelma. She taught elementary band in the Baltimore County school system and played the piano and seven other instruments well enough to teach them.

Faith decided to put the church choir back together and asked Warren if he would help. So Warren came back to the church where he first started singing. Faith put the choir together. Warren sang and never stopped coming. But Faith can't come anymore.

"On the second Sunday in June of 2013, she directed a concert with the combined choirs of our church and another church she played for down near Baltimore," Warren says. "It was a wonderful production. All of it was African-

American spirituals, and she did a magnificent job. She conducted and she played, and if you didn't know she was terminal, you would never have guessed."

A month after conducting the show, on July 12, 2013, Faith died. She was 49, the same age as her grandfather, Clifton, when he passed away.

But Faith lived long enough to bring Warren home.

THE END OF THE LINE

This story almost didn't happen. One day in December 1998, when he was 80, Warren went out to clean up some leaves, and something went seriously wrong. He couldn't make it from the house to the street. He could barely walk 10 yards without sitting down.

Something was wrong with his heart and it was going to take surgery. He downplayed it. He told his family, "This is no big deal." He told them he'd take a bus to his heart surgery and someone could pick him up afterward.

Eventually Rob took him to the hospital, where they knocked him out, split open his chest, and rerouted his blood around six blocked coronary arteries. Five days later they sent him home.

But the problems had just begun.

He says, "I couldn't even get out of a chair to go the bathroom. I was just sitting around the house. I didn't watch television. I didn't read. I had no energy. I just sat there. I'd been active all my life, and I became very depressed."

Susan says, "It was right before Christmas, and on Christmas, I remember him saying, 'It would have been better if I'd just gone and died.' He lost a great deal of weight and was taking like 12 different medicines, and the medicines were interacting and causing side effects.

"He thought he would just bounce back, but in his recovery, I had to take him to the emergency room three times."

His heart's rhythm was out of whack. When the medicine didn't work, they tried shocking his heart. When the first session didn't work, they shocked it again, and this time it came around.

Warren says, "That bypass ended with a complete reversal in what was really me. I'd always been very active. I had a hard time adjusting. I had to accept the fact I couldn't do a lot of things I used to."

But eventually he got back to singing, back to Sykesville every Sunday, back to the garden, until one day, a couple years later he fell in his house and woke up on the floor. They found three more blocked arteries. They installed stents, inserted a pacemaker, and sent him home again.

Carolyn has had problems of a different sort. She's only a year and some months younger than Warren. She's had both knees replaced, one twice, the other three times. She fell in the bedroom and broke her femur, and now one of her artificial knees is attached to a rod in her leg.

She has trouble getting around. She's very quiet. I thought she was shy, but it turns out that around the time Warren's heart broke down, something may have changed inside Carolyn's brain. Susan refers to it as a mini-stroke.

"My mother used to be very talkative," Susan says. "We don't really know when something happened, but it was obvious she was very different. Her personality changed. She doesn't say anything, she doesn't ever initiate conversations."

Before his setback in spring 2014, while he was still 93 and Carolyn was 91, Warren assessed their situation with cautious pride.

He said, "We're able to live in this house and do most of the things we need to get along. We keep ourselves fed. We do a reasonable amount of housework.

"With the pacemaker, the stents, and the bypass, and a whole handful of medications, which I take routinely every day, I'm up and around and getting along pretty good. I'm 93 years old, and my kids say I'll live to be 100. I don't know about that."

At 92, without any help, he installed a dishwasher and a gas range in his kitchen, although he admitted it wore him out a lot more than he'd expected. At 93, he still walked the treadmill every day for 15 minutes, watched "Jeopardy" and got most of the answers right, watched the news and the Orioles and generally fell asleep somewhere around the third inning.

He still mowed his own lawn. He still did the grocery shopping at least once a week, although Susan no longer tagged along.

He says, "I follow the ads. I look for bargains and prepare my list, and it depends upon where the sales are. If there are a lot in one particular place, I wait until I need several items there and then I go."

Carolyn says, "He's a penny-pincher."

Warren laughs. He says, "I've always done that. There was a time when I needed every penny I could get hold of."

And then in 2014, in late winter or early spring, it started. His blood pressure would plummet. He'd find himself on the floor. Everything exhausted him.

They tried and failed to put a new pacemaker in. A week later, they tried again and got it right, but that didn't work so well, either, at least not immediately. Eventually, they resorted to shock treatment, and after three or four weeks of what Warren refers to as "going to hell and back," things seemed to stabilize.

He knows they can't last forever, but there's no harm in trying. It's October 2014 and he's back on the treadmill. No doubt next spring he'll head out to the garden with a tilling machine.

"In winter, I'm just looking forward to when the weather warms up and the ground dries out," he says. "And I'll get my ground worked up and start gardening again. I like to see stuff grow. It's a part of me, and when the springtime comes, I need to get out and put some seeds in the ground.

"I think every year, it may be my last time, but I start again."

And he says this, too, without anything that sounds like regret or sadness, just matter-of-fact.

"There are no grandchildren. When we die, that's the end of the line."

CARRIE'S FOOTPRINTS

Carrie developed a system and a philosophy and dealt with life as it was, not how she wanted it. She wanted her kids to have a better life than hers. She wasn't educated, but she believed in education and did everything she could to make sure her kids got one.

Thelma taught school in Baltimore some 25 years and spent another 17 as a principal. Rosie taught school in Frederick and Baltimore and eventually retired and became the principal of a private religious school. Thelma's daughter, Edna, taught school in Baltimore and became a principal.

Russell's oldest girl, Rosalie, taught school in Baltimore and became a principal. Warren taught school in Frederick County and became a principal. Chester's daughter Patsy spent more than 40 years teaching. Clifton's daughter Eliza taught until she retired.

Clifton, Vernon, Everett, Russell, Romulus, and Chester were born just a bit too early. There was no high school, or they might have made it, too. Chester, Vernon, Everett, and Romulus all worked at Springfield as cooks at one time or another. Rom ended up cooking at Henryton. Vernon moved on from Springfield to the box factory. Turns out he was a wizard who could do alone and faster what typically took two men, and make good money in the process.

Chester never left Springfield till he retired. Everett did hard physical labor on the railroad till he was crushed unloading giant bales of paper, spent several weeks in the hospital, and could never work the railroad again. He spent the rest of his life cooking at Springfield.

Russell spent 20 years with the railroad, took a manufacturing job with Western Electric, and eventually moved on to Waverly Press in Baltimore, where he worked till he retired.

Mae worked as a psychiatric assistant at Spring Grove Hospital. Catherine worked cleaning houses for white people.

In Warren's immediate family, Carolyn has a bachelor's degree. Warren has a bachelor's and a master's. Glenn has degrees in mathematics and economics. Rob has a bachelor's in anthropology, an MBA, a law degree, and a new master's in information management from the University of Maryland. Susan has her undergraduate in architecture and her MBA in business.

Warren says, "I told them when they were young, the only thing I require in school is the same thing my mother required of us. Do the best you can to learn as much as you can. That means no trifling. That means no excuse for not doing the work you're assigned. And the kids have done well."

From Yokum Purl to York Imperial

There's a cake on my computer screen. Well, a picture of a cake. It's beautiful and not made of wood, and I'm sure at some point, they ate it. Here's what it says. "Dorsey 60th Family Reunion. 2009. From Yokum Purl to York Imperial." Above the number 2009, there's a depiction of a tree, and to the left of the tree, there's a photo of Ed and Carrie, and on the other side, a photo of Ed and Carrie and all the kids at the first family reunion.

Warren's in a T-shirt, looking young and handsome and happy, and when he posed, I'm sure it never crossed his mind that someday he'd be on a cake on a computer screen. It's one of those great moments in time frozen in frosting, preserved and passed down through the ages in pixels and bits.

They've been having reunions every Labor Day forever. When they held the first in 1950, Harry Truman was President, Japan and Germany were building again from rubble, and North Korean troops swarmed into South Korea. We were going to war, and another 33,000 Americans were about to die.

It was 85 years after the Civil War. Martin Luther King, Jr., was 20, and in Alabama and Mississippi and lots of other places, if you were black, you couldn't vote, you couldn't look a white man in the eye, or do much about it if they decided to blow up your house or throw your body in a river or hang you from a tree, and you sure as hell weren't sitting near the front of the bus.

In Maryland, black kids and white kids went to separate schools, blacks weren't allowed into the University of Maryland, and you could get tossed in a jail for sitting in the wrong seat at a lunch counter on Route 1, as Mae's son Wesley and his future wife, Pat Starr, did with some other kids in 1962.

Emerson and Rosie came up with the idea. Get the whole family together. Bring your own food, bring your own chairs and kids. They were all alive. Most of the grandchildren were already born.

No one had far to travel. Catherine, Carrie, and Ed were still in the old house. Vernon, Everett, Chester, and Clifton lived with their families on the hill. Warren and Emerson came in from Frederick. Thelma, Russell, Rosie, and Mae came in from Baltimore. Rom came from Marriottsville.

They turned the stable where Ed used to beat the neighbors at eightball into a makeshift reunion hall and dance floor. They gathered under an old tree just off the kitchen. They ate and played games and laughed and decided every year on Labor Day, they would do it again.

The next year they ditched the idea of bringing their own food and made food for everyone right at the reunion. Lots of chicken and potatoes and corn. Each year they got more organized. They assigned a president, a food committee, a games committee. Everyone paid dues. They played volleyball and badminton and had all kinds of races. They chose up sides and played softball by the old dump where the Giants used to play.

Eventually, a tree limb smashed the old pool hall and they had to tear it down. Sometime in the seventies, they built their own reunion center right beside Chester and Minnie's place. It's nothing fancy, small and squat and rectangular, not much more than cinder blocks painted green. One of Warren's nephews laid all the blocks.

And every year they come. They come from Iowa and Arizona and New York. They come from Frederick and Baltimore and all over Maryland. They come from Virginia and D.C., and in the case of 72-year-old Romulus Dorsey, Jr., they come from Chicago. Frances, Vivian, and Agnes, Clifton's three daughters-in-law, come up the hill or around the corner.

And, of course, Minnie just steps out the front door and comes a few feet across the lawn. For 100 years, Dorseys have lived in Sykesville, and Minnie's been there since nearly the beginning.

The fiftieth reunion in 1999 was a big one. By then Carrie, Ed, Vernon, Rom, Clifton, Everett, and Russell were gone. But the rest were there, all the girls, Catherine, Mae, Thelma, and Rosie, along with the three youngest boys, Warren, Emerson, and Chester. And yeah, they weren't girls and boys anymore. Warren was finishing out his seventies. Thelma was 88.

Jonathan Herman was mayor, and he gave Thelma a key to the town.

Ten years later, on the sixtieth anniversary, the one with the cool cake, Thelma was gone now, they were all gone, except three, and the town honored the family again. Mayor Mike Miller proclaimed Labor Day "Dorsey Reunion Day" in Sykesville, and Town Councilman Leo Keenan read the proclamation inside the Dorsey Family Reunion building.

Curt Anderson, a state delegate from Baltimore, read a proclamation from Governor Martin O'Malley honoring the Dorsey's rich heritage. The building was packed with Dorseys of every age from 93 to younger than one.

They husked 144 ears of corn. And Warren stood in front of the family and explained the thing about the Yokum Purl and the York Imperial.

He said, "At the back of our house, right outside the kitchen, there was a big apple tree, and all our young days, we thought it was a yokum purl, because that's what my mother called it, the yokum purl apples.

"But she was going on what she thought she heard people call it. And we all thought that's what it was. It wasn't till I was older and could read a bit that I discovered it wasn't a yokum purl, it was a York Imperial apple."

He referred to himself and his siblings as the 12 tribes of Ed and Carrie, and labeled the years between 1920 and 1950 as the Yokum Purl period, and 1950 onward as the York Imperial period.

There've been four or five reunions since that one, or even more, depending on when you're reading this.

Reflecting back on that sixtieth reunion in the nice family newsletter that his niece, Regine, produces, Warren wrote:

"My grandmother was a slave. The community where she lived afterwards was primarily illiterate, and at the sixtieth family reunion, there were over 200 of us, and I looked out over that multitude of Dorseys, and I could see a niece who was awarded a degree in medicine from Johns Hopkins, nephews who are engineers, people in nursing, a lot of teachers, and just about any profession you can think of. And to come from where we came and look at all them on that day, that was thrilling for me.

"If Carrie could see her family today, if she could see the 200 Dorseys at that reunion with their law degrees, MBAs, and doctorates, if she could learn of all the teachers and principals and men and women of great stature and standing no longer daunted, betrayed, or intimidated by the white world, if she could see the black President of the United States, she would know that she did not sacrifice in vain. And that her son Warren still loves her and thanks her with all his heart.

"Every one of us who claims to be a Dorsey is one of Carrie's footprints. As footprints of this humble woman, all of us share in embracing her legacy and moving the Dorsey machine forward. We must never falter, forever seeking new challenges. Carrie lit the Dorsey torch; her footprints must keep the flame glowing."

You Can Believe Them Cherries

I'm listening to an old recording. The woman on the recording is very nice. You can tell. It's a short clip, about a minute.

The voice belongs to Carrie. She must be 75 or so. At this point maybe she has the cancer, but if she knows, or if she's suffering, there's no sign in her laugh or her voice.

It's Christmas, 1961. She's with her family at Warren's house. He has an old-fashioned tape recorder, the kind with reels of spinning tape. There's a lot of hissing in the beginning and other voices in the background, and I can't make it all out, but I know she says this.

"I have really enjoyed this Christmas, if I never enjoy another one. And I say that every year. And I hope I can see next year." She meant that literally. Apparently she was having problems with her eyes and maybe developing cataracts.

Then she says something I can't make out, followed by, "You can believe them cherries." She stops at that point and laughs a big laugh, and says, "I can read everything coming down the road."

And Warren's recorder whirs and spins. There's a bit of hiss and a few more words and laughter in the background and then the tape clicks dead.

She did see the next year, but she never made it back to Frederick for Christmas again. Soon there would be nine bad months and a long line of cars moving in procession with lights on through the roads away from Sykesville.

There'd be shovels and dirt and a hole in the ground in the earth of old Bush Park.

But Warren caught her last Christmas visit on tape, and still today, you can hear Carrie laughing on Christmas 1961.

"You can believe them cherries."

"I can read everything coming down the road."

Warren says, "She was the most gallant woman I have ever seen. She sacrificed everything. She sacrificed her physical beauty. She sacrificed her general health. She would sacrifice anything for her children."

EPILOGUE

I'm on my hands and knees. The temperature's in the fifties. The wind blows. The trees shake. Crumbling leaves skitter across the grass. The sun drops through the branches to the west. The grass is pale green and thick. My fingernails are full of dirt, and I'm digging at the ground in search of the third D.

If you leave Sykesville and drive south on Route 97 a-while, you'll pass a big modern school named Bushy Park Elementary, but if you take a different route, and don't quite make it to the school, if you get just a bit away from the giant houses built on farmland in recent years, you'll come to Cemetery Road and Bushy Park Cemetery, and there you'll find about 85 graves.

Most are old. Some are new. Some have photographs adhered to the stone. One shows the face of a black boy who died in 2003. He was 18, and etched into the stone, one on each side of the boy's photograph, are pictures of

Winnie the Pooh bouncing a ball, and the words, "Mommy's Pooh Bear."

All the faces in the photos are black, and all the bones in the ground, whatever their color, are the bones of black Americans. The graveyard's filled with Dorseys. Ed's family was named Dorsey. So was Carrie's, but it's possible all these other Dorseys aren't related to Warren at all. There's Ada M. Dorsey with her stone snapped in two and lying flat on the ground. Born 1888, died 1906.

There's Vania Dorsey Greene, 1882 to 1939. There's John H. Dorsey born in 1867, and his wife, Leeanna, born in 1872. There's Robert Dorsey born in 1916 and died in 1916.

And there's this one: Dorsey, Catherine 1847–1923, John T. 1837–1918. That's Aunt Kitty and her husband, John, Carrie's parents.

I look for the blocks with the Ds on them. I find a couple. Each sticks out an inch above ground, mostly swallowed in earth and barely visible above the grass. Each is of rough concrete with an uneven top, worn and showing no sign of a D.

I can't find the third or fourth ruined D. Either someone has stolen them, time has destroyed them, or the earth has swallowed them. Then, just as I'm about to give up, I feel it.

Deep in the ground, just a bump, something hard on the grass, and I dig till I uncover the third D, except there is no D, and nature has broken down most of the block. It's hard to distinguish from the hard mud on top of it, but it's undoubtedly the decayed remains of one of Ed Dorsey's Ds.

Now I just need the fourth. I measure the distance from the second to the third with my shoes. I get 16. I go over to the first D and count off 16 to where I assume the fourth should be. I pull up grass. The ground's cool and moist. My fingers are green and filthy. And I hit it, completely grown over. I dig it free.

I uncover it, brush it clean, photograph it. I think maybe this is the first time anyone's touched these blocks since Ed gave orders while Warren and Chester dug into the ground in the weeks when Hitler's armies terrorized Europe.

I walk above the earth where Warren's parents lie. There are trees all around and graves and grass and no traffic and no sign of humanity, or even life. No squirrels, no birds, no insects, nothing except me and the blocks and the stones.

The sun's a blazing orange beyond the trees. And this cemetery and all around it, if we don't want to go all the way back to Africa, or some wretched ship crossing the sea with a bottom full of sick and frightened slaves, this is where it all began.

This is where Ed and Carrie met and started their journey. This is where they ended it, too. And this is where we'll end our story.

As I write these words, Carolyn is 92. Warren is just about to turn 94, with a fancy new pacemaker and a brand new lead shooting pulses to his heart. But like his blood pressure, his health is up and then it's down. One day he's feeling fine, the next he's faint and groping for a chair or taking another trip to the emergency room where they'll tell him he's got to give it time, until eventually they resort to shocking his heart till it agrees once more to keep on beating.

He says he's on the road to recovery. And probably he is, but nonetheless, the time has come. I wrote this fast. It's been exactly a year since I started. I'm sure it could be re-organized and expanded and changed in countless ways to make it better.

But that's too bad. Life's messy, and if this story's messy, well, that's fine. It's time to call it a book. It's time to end the story the way it is.

So here you go, Warren. Hold it in your hands. It's been a lot of fun.

In Memorium

On January 26, 2015, nearly 3 months after the initial publication of this book, Mae Dorsey Whiten passed away. She was 95.

THE DORSEY FAMILY

Ed & Carrie Dorsey

Clifton
1903-1953

Everett
1907-1975

Russell
1908-1997

Thelma
1911-2000

Romulus
1913-1961

Vernon
1915-1979

Chester
1917-2005

Mae
1919-2015

Warren
1920-

Emerson
1922-2000

Catherine
1925-2002

Rosie
1926-

Dorsey Family Quick Facts

Carrie E. Dorsey

BORN: 1886
DIED: 1963
MARRIAGE: Edward M. Dorsey, ca. 1903
MOTHER: Catherine Dorsey 1847-1923
FATHER: John T. Dorsey 1837-1918

Edward M. Dorsey

BORN: 1884
DIED: 1980
MARRIAGE: Carrie E. Dorsey, ca. 1903
MOTHER: Georgianna Savoy Dorsey
FATHER: Andrew Dorsey

James Clifton Dorsey

NICKNAMES: Cliff, Slim
BORN: December 17, 1903
DIED: March 11, 1953
MARRIAGE: Sarah Norris
CHILDREN: James, Donald, Bernice, Hazel, Thelma, Sedonia, Delmar, Eliza, Mae, Calvin, Grayson, Laura

Everett Carlton Dorsey, Sr.

BORN: February 5, 1907

DIED: 1975
MARRIAGE: Isabelle
CHILDREN: E. Carlton, Jr.., Leslie, Charles, Warren, Joan, Carrie, Howard

Russell Seward Dorsey
BORN: November 15, 1908
DIED: April 12, 1997
MARRIAGE: Marjorie
CHILDREN: Rosalie, Shirley, Janet, Betty

Thelma Georgianna Dorsey Jackson
BORN: May 24, 1911
DIED: July, 2000
MARRIAGE: Samuel Jackson, 1933
CHILDREN: Edna
EDUCATION: Dunbar High School; Douglass High School; Coppin Normal School; BS: Morgan State College; MA: New York University

Romulus David Dorsey
NICKNAME: Rom
BORN: May 20, 1913
DIED: July 4, 1961
MARRIAGE: Gladys
CHILDREN: Romulus Jr.

Vernon Langford Dorsey

BORN: April 25, 1915
DIED: August 1979
MARRIAGE: Elizabeth
CHILDREN: Polly, Peola, Betsinda, Dolly

Chester Edward Ivan Dorsey, Sr.

NICKNAME: Ches
BORN: May 6, 1917
DIED: March 17, 2005
MARRIAGE: Minnie Catherine Bond, 1941
CHILDREN: Chester Jr., Patsy, Russell

Mae Emma Selina Dorsey Whiten

NICKNAME: Sis
BORN: July 17, 1919
DIED: January 26, 2015
MARRIAGE: Harry Whiten
CHILDREN: H. Wesley, Dorothy, Verna, Martin
EDUCATION: Robert Moton High School

Warren Gamaliel Dorsey

NICKNAME: Tom
BORN: November 17, 1920
MARRIAGE: Carolyn Baugh, 1946
CHILDREN: Glenn, Robin, Susan

EDUCATION: Robert Moton High School; BS: Morgan State College; MA: Goucher College; also studied at Johns Hopkins, Loyola, and University of Maryland

Emerson Lavine Dorsey, Sr.

NICKNAME: Wee
BORN: May 11, 1922
DIED: June 22, 2000
MARRIAGE: Ethel Elizabeth Harris, 1944
CHILDREN: Iva, Rose, Emerson, Jr.
EDUCATION: Robert Moton High School; BS: Princess Anne College

Catherine Elizabeth Dorsey

BORN: March 30, 1925
DIED: February 2002
EDUCATION: Robert Moton High School

Rosie Ardell Dorsey Hutchinson

BORN: May 3, 1926
MARRIAGE: Paul Hutchinson, 1948
CHILDREN: Paula
EDUCATION: Robert Moton High School; BS: Bowie State College

MANY THANKS

Well, first I have to thank Warren and Carolyn Dorsey for all those hours sitting at the computer talking to me. I'd also like to thank Rob and Glenn and Susan Dorsey for their cooperation and great interviews, and Warren's niece, Emerson's daughter Rose, who provided all kinds of help keeping me and Warren in sync.

I'd like to thank my wife, Andrea White, for her encouragement and for copy editing the book, designing the cover, and handling most of the administrative and technical matters that made this book possible.

And I'd like to thank my two primary typists for listening to our interviews and putting them into Microsoft Word. That would be my mom, Anne White, and my daughter, Juliette White. Juliette also did historic research on the project and made sure I had my facts straight. If any of my facts aren't straight, she's in big trouble.

In the beginning there were some others who did some typing, but you know, I don't even remember who they were, so if you're one of them and I forgot you, forgive me; you have my gratitude.

I'd like to thank Jonathan Herman for his great work restoring the town of Sykesville, Bob Allen for his terrific articles and for introducing me to Jonathan through his writing, and Pat Greenwald who runs the old schoolhouse and introduced me to Warren.

SOURCES

Most of the information in the story came directly from Warren. Some came from Carolyn, and some came from Rob, Glenn, and Susan Dorsey. Some came from Warren's sister, Rosie, his sister-in-law, Minnie, and his brother Emerson's son, Emerson, Jr.

I used the Internet often. I read old articles from places like the *New York Times* and *Vanity Fair*, from the *Carroll County Times*, the *Sykesville Herald*, from the *Baltimore Sun* and the *Afro-American* archives. I drew from various websites, including Wikipedia, but most often from sites more specifically emphasizing specific incidents or topics. If I found something on one website, I would generally verify it on several others and refer to any books on the subject.

I also watched several videos and movies (which I won't list) and read many books about the Civil Rights movement or important black Americans such as Joe Louis, Jackie Robinson, Medgar Evers, and Martin Luther King, Jr.

What follows is a list of books I read. In most cases, I didn't borrow from them or quote them in any way, except where explicitly mentioned in the book. I just used their stories to better understand American history and the black experience within it. I read, or listened to, most of these books in their entirety, but can't guarantee that there weren't others I'm forgetting.

Mainly, of course, I just listened to Warren.

Alexander, Michelle. *The New Jim Crow: Mass Incarceration in the Age of Colorblindness*, The New Press, 2012.

Arsenault, Raymond. *Freedom Riders: 1961 and the Struggle for Racial Justice*, Oxford University Press. Abridged edition 2011.

Barry, John M. *Rising Tide: The Great Mississippi Flood of 1927 and How it Changed America*, Simon & Schuster, 2007.

Baty, Catherine. *Images of America: Carroll County*, Arcadia Publishing, 2006.

Blackmon, Douglas A. *Slavery by Another Name*, Anchor Books, 2009.

Branch, Taylor. *Parting the Waters: America in the King Years 1954-63*, Simon & Schuster, 1989.

Burn, Helen Jean. *Betsy Bonaparte*, The Maryland Historical Society, 2010.

Chafe, William H., Gavins, Raymond, and Korstad, Robert. *Remembering Jim Crow: African Americans Tell About Life in the Segregated South*, The New Press, 2001.

Cross, Charles. *Room Full of Mirrors: A Biography of Jimi Hendrix*, Blackstone Audio, 2006.

Davis, David Brion: *Inhuman Bondage: The Rise and Fall of Slavery in the New World*, Oxford University Press, 2006.

Davis, Sampson, Jenkins, George, and Hunt, Rameck. *The Pact: Three Young Men Make a Promise and Fulfill a Dream*, Riverhead Books, 2003.

Douglass, Frederick. *My Bondage and My Freedom*, A Public Domain Book provided by Amazon Digital Services, 2012.

Du Bois, W. E. B. *The Souls of Black Folk*, Barnes & Noble Books, 2003.

Gaines, Ernest J. *The Autobiography of Miss Jane Pittman*, Blackstone Audio, Inc., 2005.

Glaubman, Richard and Dawson, George. *Life is So Good*, Random House Publishing Group, 2000.

Goodwin, Doris Kearns. *Team of Rivals: The Political Genius of Abraham Lincoln*, Simon & Schuster, 2005.

Gordon-Reed, Annette. *The Hemingses of Monticello*, W.W. Norton & Company, 2009.

Greenberg, Linda F. *Sykesville Past & Present: A Walking Tour*, Brinkmann Publishing, 2012.

Haley, Alex. *The Autobiography of Malcolm X*, Ballantine Books, 1973.

Hall, Bill. *Images of America, Sykesville*, Arcadia Publishing, 2001.

Ifill, Sherrilyn A. *On the Courthouse Lawn: Confronting the Legacy of Lynching in the Twenty-first Century*, Beacon Press, 2007.

Jaspin, Elliot. *Buried in the Bitter Waters*, High Bridge 2007.

Margolick, David. *Elizabeth and Hazel: Two Women of Little Rock*, Yale University Press, 2011.

McBride, James. *The Color of Water: A Black Man's Tribute to His White Mother*, Riverhead Books, 2006.

McKinstry, Carolyn Maull with George, Denise. *While the World Watched*, Tyndale House Publishers, Inc., 2011.

Merrill, Philip J. and Aiono, Uluaipou-O-Malo. *Black America Series: Baltimore*, Arcadia Publishing, 1999.

Moody, Anne. *Coming of Age in Mississippi*, Dell, 2011.

Moore, Wes. *The Other Wes Moore: One Name Two Fates*, Spiegel & Grau, 2011.

Northup, Solomon. *Twelve Years a Slave*, Start Classics, 2013.

O'Brien, M.J. *We Shall Not be Moved: The Jackson Woolworth's Sit-In and the Movement It Inspired*, University Press of Mississippi, 2013.

Powell, Colin. *My American Journey*, Random House Audio, 2006.

Rediker, Marcus. *The Slave Ship: a Human History*, Tantor Audio, 2007.

Roberts, Randy. *Joe Louis: Hard Times Man*, Yale University Press, 2010.

Robinson, Jackie and Duckett, Alfred. *I Never Had It Made: An Autobiography of Jackie Robinson*, HarperCollins, 2013.

Salter, John R. Jr. *Jackson Mississippi: An American Chronicle of Struggle and Schism*, University of Nebraska Press, 2011.

Skloot, Rebecca. *The Immortal Life of Henrietta Lacks*, Crown, 2010.

Smith, C. Fraser. *Here Lies Jim Crow: Civil Rights in Maryland*, Johns Hopkins University Press, 2008.

Stowe, Harriet Beecher. *Uncle Tom's Cabin*, A Public Domain Book provided by Amazon Digital Services, 2012.

Taylor, Mildred. *Roll of Thunder Hear My Cry*, Listening Library, 2005.

Warner, Nancy M. *Carroll County Maryland, History 1837–1976*, Carroll County Bicentennial Committee, 1976.

Wilkerson, Isabel. *The Warmth of Other Suns*, Vintage Books, 2011.

Wright, Richard. *Black Boy*, Harper Perennial Modern Classics, 1997.

Yetman, Norman R. *When I Was a Slave: Memoirs from the Slave Narrative Collection*, Dover Publications, 2002.

47754749R00157

Made in the USA
Middletown, DE
01 September 2017